ENGLISH RECUSANT LITERATURE
1558–1640

Selected and Edited by
D. M. ROGERS

Volume 214

The Treasure of Vowed Chastity
in Secular Persons
1621

The Treasure of Vowed Chastity
in Secular Persons
1621

The Scolar Press
1974

ISBN 0 85967 198 4

Published and printed in Great Britain by
The Scolar Press Limited, 59-61 East Parade,
Ilkley, Yorkshire and
39 Great Russell Street,
London WC1

1825251

NOTE

Reproduced (original size) from a copy in the library of Stonyhurst College, by permission of the Rector.

References: Allison and Rogers 827; STC 15524.

THE
TREASVRE
OF VOWED
CHASTITY

in secular Persons.

-Also the

WIDDOWES
GLASSE.

VVritten by the R R. Fathers Leonard
Lessius , and Fuluius Androtius ,
both of the Society of Iesus.

Translated into English by
I. W. P.

Permissu Superiorum , 1621.

TO THE
HONORABLE
AND RIGHT
Vertuous Gentlewomā,
M^rs. Anne Vaux.

ONORABLE,
AND RIGHT
VVORTHY,
The constant
report of your vertuous

THE EPISTLE

life, in the State where-
of this little Booke entre-
ateth, hath inuited me to
entitle the same vnto
your Name in particuler,
which was written for
the profit of all in generall, who haue a true de-
fire to imbrace the State
of vowed Chastity, and
yet remaine in the world
among fecular perfons.

It the fubiect feeme
new, or ftrange to any,
I doubt not, but hauing
atten-

attentiuely read, & con-
fidered the feuerall paffa-
ges therein, they will remaine abundantly fatif-
fyed . For it was no part
of the Authors intention
(who is knowne to be fa-
mous, both for learning
and piety) thereby to de-
rogate frō other Stats of
life ; but rather, by fhew-
ing the good, & commo-
dity, which may proceed
by imbracing of this ;
thofe that be more per-

fect

THE EPISTLE

fect in themselues, might heerby, be the more honoured, and reuerenced of all.

Neither, indeed, is there any thing at al proposed in this ensewing Discourse, which hath not been practised in the Primitiue Church, by persons of both sexes; & for that cause so much admired, and extolled by the auncient Fathers of those dayes: Howsoeuer tho

DEDICATORY.

the same may seeme not to haue beene in some later ages, so much in vse, and therefore thought now behoofefull to be again renewed to our memory, in these tymes of so great necessity, for the spirituall good of soules, and increase of Charity, now halfe extinguished in the Christian world.

The profit that may, & doth redound to such

*4   as

as defire to practife this
ftate of vowed Chaftity,
remaining in the world,
will neither be fmall, or
vncertaine, if the fame
be imbraced with that
fincerity of hart and ver.
tuous manner of life as it
ought : wherein I know
your felfe to haue made
good proofe, thefe many
years, by reaping a plen-
tiful harueft of the fruits,
and heaping vp a maffe
of Treafure, againft the
                        com-

DEDICATORY.

comming of your heauē-
ly Spouse, to present him
withall, to the vnspea-
keable comfort and con-
solation of your soules e-
ternall Happynes.

To this little Trea-
tise, I haue adioyned the
WIDDOVVES GLASSE,
the which I humbly in-
treate you, to present, in
my Name, to your two
most worthy Sisters, who
for the long, constant, &
most exemplar professiō
of

THE EPISTLE of that noble, and worthy state of chast Widdowhood, may seeme to clayme a iust Title therunto. But I deemed not my labour in tranflating it, worthy to be prefented to so honourable Matrons, in a Dedicatory a part: not doubting but the same wilbe more grateful, comming through your handes, who are fo neere a kin vnto them, both by Nature & Grace;

seeing

DEDICATORY.

feeing Virginity , and
Widdowhood,haue euer
been accounted Sifters,
and betroathed to the
fame Eternall Spoufe
Chrift Iefus.

Accept then (Right
worthy Gentlewoman)
thefe few fheets of paper,
by me tranflated out of
Latin,as a future earneft
of fom better gift, wher-
with I intend to prefent
you ere it be long . And
in the meane tyme , a-
mongft

THE EPISTLE

mong the many of your pious and deuout exercises, forget him not, who will euer remaine

Your deuoted
seruant,

I. W.

THE

THE
GOOD AND
COMMODITY

*Of the state of life, which
some professe, liuing in
the world, and vowing
Chastity.*

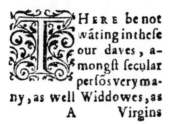

HERE be not
wanting in these
our dayes, a-
mongst secular
persos very ma-
ny, as well Widdowes, as
Virgins

A

Virgins, who aspyring to perfection, haue a desire (as farre as they may conueniently) to sequester themselues from the troubles and incombrances of the world, thereby to imploy their mindes more freely and securly in the seruice of God.

For whome notwithstanding, to liue in Monasteryes, either it is not so cōuenient, or els (grounded vpon sufficiét reasons) they may be otherwise resolued. For the wayes & manners of seruing God are diuers, & those who cannot aspire

to

to the highest & most perfect, are not therefore constrayned to content themselues with the meanest & least noble.

Wherfore many there be who liuing in the world, reiecting the vanity of rich and costly apparell, and taking a plaine & simple habit, consecrate their Virginity to Almighty God; and auoyding the conuersation of secular persons (as much as they may) do imploy themselues wholy in the offices of Charity and Deuotion.

Yet neuerthelesse, be-

cause there be not wanting
som, who (I know not out
of what zeale) carpe at the
Inſtitution of ſuch manner
of life, I am for this reſpect
wonne, at the intreaty of a
ſpecial friend, to declare out
of holy Scripture, and ancient Fathers, in what degree ſuch kind of life in the
Catholike Church is to be
eſteemed : for the ſatisfacti-
on of whom in a matter of
ſuch importance, and ſo
much pertayning to the
good of ſoules, I haue pur-
poſed to handle it in eight
little Chapters following,
                    where

where, in the first, it is proued out of holy Scripture,
that this kind of life is pious and laudable.

In the second, the same
is proued by Exáples out of
holy Scripture, and Ecclesiasticall historyes.

In the third, the same is
conuinced by the Authori-
tyes of holy Fathers.

In the fourth, the same is
confirmed by Theologicall
Arguments.

In the fifth, the same is
also confirmed out of the
good & commodity which
ensue of Chastity.

A 3 The

The sixt, contayneth a solution to certaine obiections made, concerning the merits of Marriage & Chastity.

The seauenth, setteth downe certaine admonitions & aduices, to be exactly followed in this estate.

The eight, sheweth that this manner of life, is truly and properly called an Estate.

CHAP.

CHAP. I.

VVherin it is proued out of Scrip-
ture, that, that kind of life,
wherin ſome, Men or VVomē,
liuing in the world, leauing of
coſtly apparrell, & vſing plain
and modeſt attire, doe vow
Chaſtity, is laudable and me-
ritorious before God.

THERE be many in
this age who vſing o-
uer much the liberty of
their owne Iudgments, dif-
allow of this kind of life:
yet by what reaſons, or v-
pon what grounds they are
moued ſo to do, beſids thoſe
A 4   which

which *Iouinian* the ancient
heretike (& thefe alfo of his
coate euen in thefe tymes)
hath alleadged, I cannot i-
magine. Neither do I think
they haue any other, vnles
perhaps they confider the
difficulties which this mā-
ner of life is fubiect vnto, &
are terrifyed with more
dangers of liuing chaft in
this, then in the ftate of religion . For which caufe
they may thinke it more fe-
cure to vow Chaftity in the
one, then in the other . But
neuerthelesse it is to be held
as a point of faith, that this
State

State is not only lawful, but
also commendable, and of
great merit before Almighty God; and the same pra-
ctised not only of men, and
women, but also of youth
it selfe.

This is euidently con-
uinced out of holy Scrip-
tur, wher our Lord himself
(*Matth* 19.) doth openly cō-
mend this Institution. For
first when the Apostls hea-
ring the speaches of our
Blessed Sauiour cōcerning
Marriage, answered, *Si ita
est &c.* If such be the condition of man, linked vnto a
vvife

wife (to wit, that it is lawfull to haue but one, neither
to be so separated from that
one, that whiles she liues he
may take another) it is better not to marry, & incurre
such a seruitude. To whom
our Lord replyed, appro-
uing that which they had
sayd: *Non omnes capiunt &c.*
al apprehed not this speach
but only such to whome it
is giuen: for there be those
who haue made themselues
Eunuches for the kingdom
of heauen &c. He who can
~~vnderstand~~ this, let him
vnderstand it.

Heere

Heere our Lord spake
of single life in generall,
commending the same also
in those who liue in the
world; first, when appro-
uing the answere of his
aforesayd Apostles (who
then thought not of liuing
in Monasteryes, or being
Religious) he sayd: *Non omnes capiunt &c.* All apprehend
not this word; as though
he should haue sayd, you
rightly infer, that it is not
conuenient to marry, but
few there be who vnder-
stand a thing of so great, &
high a Mystery.

Second-

Secondly, when diftin-
guifhing three forts of Eunuches, he fheweth, that
thofe do greatly pleafe him,
who haue made themfelues
Eunuches, that is to fay,
who haue exempted them-
felues from Marriage, for
the Kingdome of heauen:
To wit, that being thereby
made more free, from the
burthen of fuch a clogge,
they may runne the fafter
vnto it, and enioy it more
fafely and aboundantly.

Thirdly when he faith,
He that can vnderftãd this
myftery, let him vnderftãd
it

it : as if he should haue said,
I constraine no man, but ex-
hort al, for it is a great bene-
fit to abstaine from mariage
for the kingdome of God .
Therefore he who hath so
great a courage, that he ho-
peth he shalbe able to apre-
hend & imbrace so great a
good, let him not neglect it.

Wherefore since our
Lord did not only comend
this state in generall , but
also in particuler according
to which the apostles vnderstood him, & which might
haue been practized at that
tyme ; it followeth manife-
B   stly

ftly, that the same is commendable, and most acceptable vnto God, being practised also by those that liue in the world.

Neither can it be said, that our Lord spake not of the vow of Chastity, but onely of the simple purpose and vse therof: for to be made an Eunuch, is not only to abstaine from Mariege, but also to bereaue ones selfe of al ability therof, and of all other carnall pleasure; which is done in effect also, by the vow of Chastity. For euen as the corporall

corporall making one an
Eunuch, cuts off all sufficiency of carnall act, or delight: So likewise the spirituall making one an Eunuch, which is effected by
the vow of chastity, disinables al morall faculty so farre, that we may not vse any
such delight lawfully, making it morally impossible
(as it is incompatible with
Iustice) to do it. For what
we cannot lawfully do,
may be absolutely said, that
we cannot do, and is said to
be (iustly) impossible.

From whence it is, that
holy

holy Fathers vsually out of
this place of Scripture proue the vow of Chastity, because a spirituall making
one an Eunuch, cannot be
otherwise effected, then by
vow. See *S. Augustine* in his
booke of holy Virginity .
cap. 30. *S.Hierom* in his book
against *Iouinian* , and vpon
this place of S . Matthew
cap. 19 . The same is cleerly
proued out of the Apostle 1.
Corinth . 7. where he greatly
prayseth singlenes of life ,
professed in diuers manners
of estate , and obserued also
in the world, and in priuat
howses

howses , for as then Monasteryes were not yet begun .
Dico innuptis &c. I speak both
to the vnmaried, & to Widdowes , that it is good for
thē to remain in that estate,
as I haue also done. And a-
gaine: *I would haue al be as I my*
selfe, that is, I desire that all
should be continēt, as it wil
appeare out of that which
follows. *De Virginibus &c.* As
for those that are virgins, I
haue no expresse commissi-
on to them from our Lord,
but I giue them Counsell
(to wit, that they remain in
their Virginity) as hauing
B 3   obtayned

obteyned mercy of Almighty God, to be faithfull, &c. And againe, *Si nupserit virgo &c* : If a virgin marry, she sinneth not, but such notwithstanding shal haue the tribulation of the flesh, that is to say, many troubls cares, and afflictions &c. Againe: *Igitur qui &c*. Therfore he which giueth a virgin in mariage, doth well, but he which doth it not, doth better. Also, *Beatior erit &c*. she shalbe more happy if she remaine so still (to wit vnmarried) according vnto my aduice, for I think
that

that euen I my selfe, haue the spirit of God. In al these places the Apostle comends the loue of Chastity, and Virginity, eué in the world and in priuate howses, as it was obserued at that tyme.

For in Ancient tymes, when the faithfull were most deuout, many followed the aduice of our Sauiour, in such manner, as they had then oportunity to do it, as is manifest out of the Acts of the Apostles; where many hauing sould their goods & bestowed the money in common, imbraced

B 4   pouerty

pouerty. It is very probable
therfore, that there were a
greater nûber of those who
imbraced Chastity , then
others , both becaufe that
vertue was more noble and
profitable , and alfo becaufe
there might be many poore
folks which had not goods
and poffeffions to fell , or if
they had, yet perhaps could
not fell them ; all   which
notwithftanding   might
profeffe Chastity.

Neither is it to be doub-
ted, but that many obliged
themfelues by vow there-
unto,fince they imbraced it
out

out of a desire of perfection
and zeale to pleale Almi-
ghty God. And it. is more
perfect a great deale to keep
it with an entire relolutiõ,
then only with an vncer-
taine and mutable purpole.

Finally allo, becaule they
imbraced it out of the mo-
tiue of our Sauiours owne
aduife and commendation
therof; and that which our
Sauiour cõmended was the
voluntary making of them-
felues Eunuches, which is
effected by vow, as hath bin
faid before. The fame is col-
lected allo out of the A-
poftle

poſtle 1. *Tim.* 5. *Adoleſcentiores viduas &c.* Take none of the younger ſort of widowes, &c. which is meant that they ſhould not be admitted into the function or miniſtery of *diaconiſſes*, or into the number of the *Alumnæ* or *Pupills* of the Church. *Cùm enim &c.* for that, ſaith *S. Paul*, after they haue liued licentiouſly in Chriſt, at laſt alſo they will not ſticke to marry, fruſtrating their former Faith : that is, they will breake the vow of Chaſtity which they had made before; for the word *Fayth*, is

taken

taken in this place for *Promise*, or obligation dew by promise: as for example, to *give* ones *Faith*, is to giue ones promise, to *keepe fayth*, is to keepe promise, to *frustrate fayth* giuen before, is to breake promise, and a promise made to God, is a vow.

From hence it is manifest, that it was a custom in the primitiue Church, for Widdowes also to vow Chastity, so that without a mortall sin; & being guilty of damnation, they could not marry againe: besides that

that, euery act of Concu-
piscence, yea and the very
marriage it self was iniury
against Christ; for so much
is signified in these words,
After they haue liued licentiously
in Christ, that is to say, after
they haue liued lasciuiously
and luxuriously, wron-
ing our Sauiour Christ,
to whome they had bound
themselues by vow, and
were become espowsed to
him, at length also they
will not sticke to marry.
After this manner the Cou-
cell of *Carthage* the 104. *Ca-*
non, and S. *Chrysostome* vpon
this

this place, and *S. Hierome* in his epistle to *Herontia de Monogamia*, and other ▮▮ do expound it.

This place is to be noted & pondered of all such as haue made vow to Almighty God of perpetuall Chastity, for that without being guilty of eternall damnation, they can neither marry (especially with an intention to consummate) nor otherwise enioy carnal delight, which also is the opinion of all the Fathers, who interprete this place to be of promise made vnto

C   God

God, & the vow of Chasti-
ty.

Fina, wheresoeuer ho-
ly Scripture commendeth
Virginity, it speaketh in generall; neither is it to be restrained vnto those alone,
who liue in Monasteryes.
And all rewards and priui-
ledges of Virginity there
rehearsed, belong vnto all
holy Virgins, as in the 3.
chap. of the Booke of *VVise-*
dome: Foelix est sterilis &c. happy is she that is barren and
vndefiled , which neuer
knew any impure bed, she
shall haue fruite in the be-
houl-

houlding of foules that are
blessed &c. *Apoc*. 14. It is
granted only vnto Virgins
(*sequi Agnum quocumq; ierit*) to
follow the Lambe where-
foeuer he goeth, and to fing
that new Hymne in *Isay* 56.
To Eunuches which keep
Gods diuine Commande-
ments, is promifed an e-
uerlafting name, and a high
place, and a degree in the
Citty of Almighty God.

Some will obiect that,
that place of the Apoftle 1.
Tim. 5. faying : *Volo iuniores
nubere &c.* I would haue the
younger fort to marry, to

bring forth Children and
keep house &c. makes cleare
againſt that which we haue
ſayd. To this I anſwere,
that it is not to be vnder-
ſtood of all Widdowes that
are young, but only of thoſe
which cannot liue conti-
nent, and are not otherwiſe
obliged by any vow : for it
is better that ſuch ſhould
marry, then liue inconti-
nent, and giue ſcandall to
the vnfaythfull, as the A-
poſtle inſinuateth in the
ſame place.

Alſo the holy Father S.
Chryſoſtome in his 15. *Homily*
                              vpon

vpon the 1. to *Timothy*, affirmeth, that the Apostle speaketh there of such widows,
who being freed from the
yoake and gouernement of
their husbands, liue disso-
lutly, become idle, pratlers,
wanton, curious, running
vp and down to their nei-
ghbours houses, & the like.
And it is manifest out of the
text it selfe that the Apostle
speaketh of such, when he
sayth: *Volo &c.* I would haue
the younger sort to marry.
S. Ambrose also in his booke
of *VViddowes* explicateth *S.*
Paul. Pro remedio suasit nuptias
C 3 *&c.*

*&c.*he perſwaded Marriage
as a remedy, but not pre-
ſcribed it as a choice. S.
Hierome in his 8. Epiſtle to
Saluina, asking : *Cur nuptias
Paulus indulſerit &c.*Why did
S. *Paul* fauour Marriage?
Preſently he addeth: *Iam
quædam &c.* Some haue al-
ready declined after Sathá:
whereby we may vnder-
ſtand, ſayth S. *Hierome,* that
theſe ſpeaches rather ſignify
a helping hand to be lent to
thoſe that are fallen, then
the reward of a crowne·o
thoſe which ſtand firme :
See then (ſayth he) what
theſe

these second Marriages be,
which are yet to be preferred before the condition of
a Brothell-house: for some
haue declined after Sathan;
therefore a young Widdow
which cannot, or will not
containe her selfe, let her
rather take a husband then
the diuel. So S. *Hierome* Out
of which it appeares that it
is not conuenient for all
young Widdowes to mar-
ry, but onely such who
are subiect to the vices a-
boue named, to wit, in
whome there is manifest
danger of Incontinency, or
C 4   which

which cannot liue chaſt,
or will not vſe meanes to
do it.

CHAP. II.

The ſame is proued by examples
out of holy Scripture, and the
cuſtome of the Church, moſt
frequently practiſed from the
firſt beginning of Religion, euen
vnto theſe dayes.

FIRST of all, doth here
preſent her ſelfe our
bleſſed Lady, as guide and
Author of this Inſtitution,
who liuing in the world at
her owne command, and
free from being ſubiect to
any

any other , reseruing alſo
her proper goods , vowed
vnto God perpetuall virginity , & this either before ,
or immediatly after her
Marriage .

And truly , if before her
marriage (as it is moſt likely
ſhe did, and *S. Auguſtin* in his
Book of holy virginity *cap.*
4 . doth thinke moſt pro-
bable) then ſhe contracted
not a marriage afterwards of
her owne accord , but ra-
ther moued thereunto by
diuine Reuelatiō, by which
alſo ſhe was aſſured that
there ſhould be no danger
to

to loose her virginity , and
that her husbād also should
binde himselfe by the like
vow of Chastity; wherfore
she neuer consented neither
expresly, nor in effect to any
matrimoniall Act . For albeit that in the contract of
Marriage, there is power
giuen to the husband ouer
his wiues body, yet by this
reuelation she was assured
that it should in her neuer
actually take effect. And as
she for her part had chosen
to preuent it , so likewise
her husband should preset-
ly do the like .

But

But it she made her vow
after Marriage, it is to be
sayd that she contracted
Marriage, not with an ab-
solute consent to consumat
the same, but in such manner as she referred her selfe
wholy to the prouidence
of Almighty God, relying
altogeather vpon his diuin
will and pleasure. Moreo-
uer it is most manifestly probable that our Blessed Lady had vowed Chastity,
out of these wordes of S.
Luke : Quomodo fied istui &c.
How that this com to passe,
since I know not man that
is

is to fay , how fhall I con-
ceiue a Sonne, that cannct
know Man , becaufe I am
boúd by my vow of Virgi-
nity?for fo the holy Fathers
*Athanafius, ferm . de fanctiffma
Deipara, Gregory Niffin* in his
Oration on the birth cf our
Sauiour, *S. Auguftine* in his
booke of holy *Virginity cap.*
4. *S . Bernard* in his fourth
fermon *fuper miffus eft &c.* do
teach ; and reaſon it felfe
doth likewiſe manifeftly
conuince . For otherwiſe
her obiection to the Angell
had beene to no purpoſe,
fince it might haue beene
                          anſwe-

answered vnto her, Now
thou shalt know man, and
conceaue. Therefore her
obiection, *I know not man*, is
the same, *that I cannot know
man*: euen as he who hath
vowed to abstaine from
flesh or wine, being inuited
sayth: *I eate not flesh, I drinke
not wine, I frequent not banquets &c.*

An innumerable multi-
tude of Virgins presently
followed the example of
our B. Lady, in so much
that one howse, to wit of
Philip the deaco̅, had 4. daughters remayning virgins, as
D

it is manifest out of the Acts
of the Apostles *Chap.* 21.
who also were indued with
the spirit of Prophecy, as it
is there said: which as S.
Hierome witnesseth in his
Epistle to *Demetriades*, was
granted them as a reward
of their Virginity.

S. *Philip* the Apostle before his Apostleship, brought vp three daughters also,
wherof two remayned vir-
gins till they were very old
as *Policrates* in S. *Hierome* re-
porteth *De Scrip. Ecclesiast.* in
Polycrate.

S. *Petronilla* daughter S. *Peter*
vowed

vowed virginity, and for
feare of loosing it, obteyned
soden death from Almigh-
ty God.

S. *Tecla* at the perswa-
sion of *S. Paul*, imbraced the
same, as *S. Ambrose* witnesseth in his second booke
of Virgins.

S. Iphigenia daughter to
the King of *Ethiopia*, by the
counsell of *S. Matthew*, as
Abdias writeth in her life.

Flauia Domitilla daugh-
ter to *Clemens* the Consull,
& S. *Peters* host at Rome, at
the perswasion of *S. Clemēt*,
as S. *Bede* witnesseth in his

D 2   Mar-

Martyrologe the 7. of May, or as it is set downe in his life, at the perswasion of *Nereus* and *Achilleus*.

S. *Valeria* at the perswaſiõ of *S. Martialis*, as appeareth out of his Epiſtle *ad Tholoſanos*, *Chap.* 8.

S. *Pudentiana* & her ſiſter *Praxedes*, by the Counſell of the Apoſtles, or Apoſtolicall men.

Finally *S. Anatolia, Apollonia, Balbina, Barbara, Pelagia, Catherina, Cæcilia, Agatha, Agnes, Lucia, Baſilla, Chriſtina, Dorothea, Emerentiana, Priſca, Euphemia, Saturnina, Suſanna, Victo-*

Victoria, *Theodora*, and innumerable others contynued virgins, in the world, euen to their death, and honoured their virginity with the crowne of Martyrdome.

Moreouer it is manifest out of *S. Cyprian*, *S. Ambrose* & *S. Hierome* with other holy Fathers, that there were in those ages infinite who cōsecrated their virginity to Almighty God, although they entred not into Monasteries, but dwelt either in their Parents howses, or in their owne, retayning the vse of their proper

D 3 goods

goods , or els liued many
together in comon.

The same appeareth also
out of the testimony of *Fau-*
stus Manichaus in *S . Augustine* ,
in his 30. boke against *Fau-*
stus the 4. *Chap* . where *Fau-*
stus thus obiecteth. *Nec videtis*
hinc &c . Neither do you see
heere, both your virgins to
be noted of being deceaued
by the doctrine of the Diuell, and your selues to become his Prelats, who con-
tentiously alwayes incite
them to this profession, by
your perswasions, that there
is almost now in your
                    Chur-

Churches a greater number
of Virgins, then of marryed women.

By which speach two
things are to be noted, that
Bishops & Prelates, euery
where through the whole
world, did earnestly incite
those that were vnder their
charge to the profession of
Virginity, and that the nūber of those who did pu-
blikely professe Virginity,
was as great as those that
were married. See S. *Am-*
brose in his 30. booke of Virgins, where he sheweth the
same most euidently.

D 4   Amongst

Among thefe alfo ma-
ny were very eminent and
wealthy, as the daughters
of Senatours , and Prin-
ces, and many of them had
wayting women to follow
them when they went a-
broad, as it appeares out of
S. *Hierome* in his 8. Epiftle
to *Demetriades*, where he alfo warneth fuch Miftreffes,
that, as they themfelues go
modeftly in their apparell,
fo they fhould caufe their
women of attendáce alfo to
auoyd vanity in their attyres, & fee that their habits
were modeft and graue.

Be-

Besides many Fathers haue written of the attyre, and discipline of Virgins, as *Tertullian, S. Cyprian, S. Ambrose, S. Hierome,* in diuers places of their workes. All which they directed specially vnto such, as liuing out of Monasteryes at their owne gouernment; imbraced virginity. And the said holy Fathers do warne thē that they should not be seen in publique without veils, and ciuilly accompanyed; that they should not vse secular ornaments; that they should abstaine from painting

ting, and vanity in their
cloathes; that they should
auoyde vnprofitable mee-
tings, marryages and ban-
quets; that they should giue
their almes with a pure intention to the reliefe of or-
phans, and such as were in
distresse. All which things
it is manifest do belong to
such as are at their owne
disposing, and retaine their
proper substance.

Neither haue we on-
ly examples of Chastity in
single or vnmarryed folkes,
but also euen in those thé-
selues which are marryed,
which

which to auoyd tediousnes
I omit . *See Marulus in his* 4.
booke the 7. *and* 8. *chap. Fulgosus
in the* 4. *chap* . *Ignat. in his* 6.
Booke . Out of which it appeares euidently , that this
inftitution of imbracing &
profeffing Chaftity, in the
world , hath beene moft
frequent and vfuall , euer
fince the beginning of the
Church , and therefore very commendable and meri-
torious .

CHAP.

CHAP. III.

*The same is witnessed by the te-
stimonyes of holy Fathers.*

MERVAILOVS are
the commendations
which holy Fathers giue
to this state of life, which
are no lesse referred to such
as obserue it in the world,
then to those which pro-
fesse it in Monasteryes. S.
Ignatius in his epistle *ad Thar-
senses* calleth *Virgins* (so vowed vnto God) *the Priests of
Christ*, because they offer
their bodyes to God as a sa-
crifice, *Eas qua in virginitate
degunt*

degunt &c. Account, faith he, thofe, who liue in the ftate of Virginity, as Priefts of Chrift.

S. *Athanafius* in his little worke of virginity, about the end, fayth: *Magna virtus continentia &c.* Continency is a great vertue, purity is a thing worthy to be boafted of, great are the prayfes of Virgins. O Virginity, treafure inconfumable, garland neuer to be withered, temple of Almighty God, houfe of the holy Ghoft, Margarite moft pretious, ouercomer of death & hell,

E   life

life of Angels, crowne of
Saints &c. *S. Cyprian* in his
booke of the *habit and disci-*
pline of Virgins : *Nunc nobis ad*
Virgines sermo est &c. Now
speake we of Virgins, sayth
he, of whom by how much
their glory is the more eminent, by so much their care
is the greater. This is the
flower of ecclesiastical bud,
the ornament and grace of
spirituall grace it selfe, the
hopeful towardnes of praise and honour, a worke entire and vncorrupted, the i-
mage of God correspondēt
to the sanctimony of our
Lord

Lord, the more beautifull
part of Christ his flock &c.
And afterwards: *si præmium*
pollicitationis &c. If thou ex-
pect the reward of promise,
thou wilt count thy labour
little: Immortality shalbe
giuen to him, that perse-
uereth; perpetuall life is
propoled a reward; our
Lord promiseth a king-
dome:preserue yee Virgins,
preserue that which you
haue begun to be, preserue
that which yee shall be, for
great is the reward proui-
ded for you &c.

That which wee must
E 2 be

be heereafter, you haue begun to be already ; yee poffeffe in prefent the glory of
the Refurrection in the age
to come; yee paffe through
the tymes without taking
infectiō from them as long
as yee perfeuere in Chaftity
and Virginity ; yee are e-
quall euen to the Angells of
God , folide and vntoucht;
Virginity only endures , o-
nely lafteth for euer.

The firft Precept *(S. Cy-
priā* goeth ftill on) of Almighty God, commaunded to
increafe and generate; the
fecond perfwaded Conty-
nency

nency . Whilst the world was rude & vnpeopled, by our fertility , by generation we were multiplyed, & grewe to the increase of mankind : but now when the world is peopled and filled, those who are capable of Chastity are made Eunuches spiritually , after the manner of things that are made vselesse to the Sex, for the kingdome of God. Hitherto S . *Cyprian* .

S. Basill in his booke of true Virginity saith: Virginity is certainly a great and excellent thing, which ma-

E 3   keth

keth a man incorruptible
like vnto God himselfe; but
it passeth not from our bodyes into our soules : yet
being the propriety of an
incorporeall nature , keeps
also our bodyes incorrupt
with a pretious integrity
&c. Virgins haue before
hand indewed themselues
with that which by deuine
vertue, must be perfected in
vs at the Resurrection ; for
liuing heere like vnto Angells, they neither marry,
nor are marryed , but are
both in vertue of minde, &
integrity of body, equall
vnto

vnto Angells. The same Father explicating also the words of the Prophet *Esay* 56. of Eunuches, he wryteth in this manner. *Pro humano nomine &c.* Insteed of a humane name, sayth our Lord, I will giue them a name of Angells which are immortall, that they may haue heauen and the fairest part therof to remaine in, and that dwelling in the most beautiful seate of heauen, that is to say, in my house, within the inclosurs thereof, they may receaue not only the nature of the

E 4   Angels,

Angells, and the honour of
perpetuall succession, being
sufficient of themselues to
continue an eternall succession of their kind, in themselues, for life euerlasting;
but also that they may haue
a principall place amongst
Angells, and a name inde-
leble, which for the great
splendour in their beauty
shall neuer decay &c.

S. *Gregory Nazianzen* in
his Verses in the prayse of
Virginity singeth thus: *Sal-
ue Virginitas &c.*

Haile Cha*st*ity *the guift of
only Heauen,*

Parent

*Parent of a pure life, by whom
are giuen*

*Our greatest goods, part euen
of Christ, and one*

*Thats to celestiall spirits com-
panion:*

*Nor euer knew of vnchast bed
the touch,*

*For God himselfe and his faire
Quire are such.*

S. *Iohn Chrysostome* in his
booke of Virginity the *cap.*
2. sayth: Virginity so much
excells marriage, by how
much heauen doth earth,
and Angells mortall men.
And againe in the 12. *chap.*
Humanity since it is inferiour

riour to thofe happy fpirits
the Angells, as farre as it is
able, ftriueth to attaine vnto their perfection . And
how ? Angells marry not,
nor take to them wiues, no
more doth a Virgin. Angels
wayting alwayes about the
throne of Almighty God,
do ferne him : fo doth a
Virgin . Wherefore S . *Paul*
calls them away from all
cares, that they may con-
tinually imploy themfelues
in the feruice of God, without hauing wherewithall
to be diftracted. Againe,
chap. 37. Dare any one after
                        all

all this compare marriage
with virginity, or but once
bring the one in presence
of the other? S. *Paul* suffe-
reth not this, who interpo-
seth a great distance betw-
eene these two, where he
sayth: the one thinketh on
matters belonging vnto
God, the other on matters
belonging to the world.

S. *Ambrose* in his first booke
of virgins saith. *Nec immerito
&c.* deseruely hath virginity deriued from heauen the
manner of her life, since it
is in heaue that her Spouse
hath his dwelling place.

This

This clowde paffing thorough the Ayre, Skyes, & Quires of Angells themfelues, hath found out the word of God, euen in the bofome of God the Father, and hath filled its bowells therwith. For who is it, that hauing found fo great a good, will leaue it? For thy Name is an oyntment powred out, wherfore yong virgins, and maides haue loued thee, and taken thee vnto them. Finally, that is not my faying, Becaufe thofe which neither are nor wilbe marryed, fhall

be

be as the Angells of God in
heauen .

Let none therfore mer-
uaile (faith S . *Ambrose* further) that they are cõpared
to the Angells of God who
are lincked and vnited in
the God of Angells *&c*. Let
vs compare therfore the cõ-
tents of marryed women ,
with the loweſt and leaſt
happines of Virgins .

Admit (faith he further)
that fome great woman
fhould boaſt of her fertility
& the fruit which fhe hath
brought forth : by how
many the more Children
F   fhe

she hath beene deliuered of,
by so much the greater haue
beene the panges & paynes
which she endured. Let her
reckon the ioy which she
hath of her children , and
withall she may count likewise the troubles which
they haue caused her . She
marryeth and weepeth : &
what wise vowes are these,
which so sodenly must be
repented &c.

Againe . Yow haue heard
all yee that are mothers,
in what vertues , in what
order, and discipline, yee
ought to bring vp your
chil-

childré, that you may haue
some of your owne, by
whose merites your owne
sins & offences may be for-
giuen. A Virgin is one to
whom God hath giuen her
to be so, and therefore she is
his guift, she is the reward
of her Parents &c. A virgin
is the oblation of her Mother, by whose dayly sacri-
fice Gods diuine power is
appeased.

S. *Hierome* in his first
book against *Iouinian cap.* 1.
Ideo plus amat &c. Therefore
our Sauiour Christ loueth
Virgins the more, because

of

of their owne accord they
giue him that, which was
not exacted of them : and
it is a token of greater grace
to offer that which is not
due, then to giue that
which they are compelled
vnto.

And afterward : *Grandis fidei est &c.* It is a worke
of great fayth, and much
vertue, when the Temple
of God is most pure to offer
it entierly as a burnt-sacrifice vnto our Lord, and according to the Apostle to
be holy, aswell in body as
in spirit.

S. Au-

S.Augustine in his booke
of holy Virginity *cap.* 13.
sayth: Virginall integrity
is an Angelicall portion
and a perpetuall medita-
tion of incorruptibility in
a corruptible body. Let all
fertility of body giue place
vnto this, and all conti-
nency of marryed persons
yeild vnto it; for thefor-
mer is not in our owne
power, the later liueth not
in eternity. The liberty of
our will extendeth not
vnto bodily fruitfulnesse,
Matrimoniall Chastity is
not found in Heauen.

They

They certainely shall haue
some reward aboue all o-
thers in that generall immortality, who haue already growne in their flesh
somwhat that is not fleshly.
Wherefore they are much
ourseene, who thinke the
good & commodity of this
continency not to be neceffary, for the kingdome of
heauen, but onely for the
present world wherein we
liue.

In which last wordes
he conuinceth *Iouinia* & the
heretiks of our tymes, who
with him teach, that Vir-
ginity

ginity is only conuenient
to auoyd worldly troubles.

S . *Fulgentius* in his 3. E-
piſtle to *Proba* cap . 9 . *Di-
cimus à sanctis nuptijs &c.* We
affirme (wheras thoſe marry who cannot liue conti-
nent) that holy Virginity
as farre excelleth holy Matrimony, as that which is
better excelleth that which
is good, that with is high
excelleth that which is
low, that which is heauenly excelleth earthly, that
which is holy, more holy ,
mortall marriage, marriage
immortall, the fleſh the ſpi-

F 4 rit,

rit, weakenes ftrength, the
fruit of a trafitory iffue the
fruite of a braunch euerlafting, tribulation fecurity,
vnfetlednes of mind tran-
quillity, a good which is
momentary and ful of troubles excelleth that which is
better, and accompanyed
with ioy euerlafting.

These & many other
thinges, holy Fathers haue
written in the comendatió
of virginity, by which the
excellency & worth therof
may be beeter knowen and
efteemed, no one vertue or
eftate of life being comme-
ded

ded with so great affection,
& consent of holy Fathers,
as this.

Heereupon, especially
in former ages, an infinite
multitude haue imbraced
it, in so much that *S. Ambrose*
in his 3. booke of Virgins
affirmeth, That in the Easterne & Africā Churches,
there were more virgins
consecrated to Almighty
God, then wee haue men
borne in our parts heere.
And yet notwithstanding
mākind is not therby diminished, but increased. If
any one (quoth he) imagi-
neth

neth, that the number of
mankind is diminished by
the multitude of virgins,
let him consider,that where
there are few virgins there
are also the fewer persons,
and where the number of
them is more frequent who
are louers and imbracers of
Virginity, there also the
number of men is more
great. Consider how many
Alexandria, & al the Easterne
parts, with the Churches
also of Affrica, was wont
euery yeare to consecrate:
fewer men are heere begotten then there virgins con-
secra-

secrated; the reason wherof
is, that God will not be o-
uercome with liberality :
but if the Parents offer him
a Child or two, he renders
them eight or ten, graun-
ting fruitefullnes, and for-
tunate Childe-bearing to
such, as are mothers, and
filling their howses with
his blessing. Therfore euen
as faithfull paying of Ty-
thes, & liberality towards
the poore, bringeth not
pouerty, since God by his
prouidence prospereth and
increaseth our substance, &
maketh our fields the more
fruite-

fruitfull, as S. *Hierome* teacheth *Serm.* 219. *de tempore*;
fo the loue and affection to
virginity hindreth not the
world , nor wafteth the
number of fecular Perfons,
but obteyneth it a longer
benediction.

CHAP. IIII.

The fame is proued alfo, by
reafon.

THE errour of *Iouinian*
was , that Virginity
did not excell Marriage,
which he meant by virgi-
nitv, taken abfolutely and
generally, whether it were
pro-

professed by persons liuing
in the world or in Religió.
He therefore who confes-
seth that virginity professed
in the state of Religion, is
to be preferred before Marriage, but not that which
is imbraced in the world, is
at least halfe a Iouinianist,
because he is halfe of his o-
pinion; nay rather he seemes to be altogeather of
the same minde, and really
a Iouinianist, because he
denieth, that Virginity is
of it own nature better thē
Marryage, wherein the
whole Errour of Iouinian

G   about

about this matter confifted.
For if of it owne proper nature it were better, it would
followe , that the fame being alfo profeffed in the
world , would be better.
See *S. Auguftine Cap.* 28. *ad*
Quod-vult-Deum, and *S. Ierome*
in his 10. booke againft the
fame *Iouinian &c.*

If it were not làudable
and meritorious to vow
Virginity , liuing in the
world, either it fhould be
for the great difficulty and
morall impoffibility of kee.
ping their vow in that eftate, or els becaufe Chaftity

ty is not better then marri-
ag; for no other reaſon can
be imagined . Not the former, for it is an hereſy of
the heretikes of theſe our
daies, who for the difficulty
therof, affirme , that ſuch a
vow is not to be made , vnleſſe the perſon know that
he is peculiarly inſpired
with the guift of continency. Not the latter, for it is
the errour of *Iouinian* afore-
ſaid. Cõcerning the gift of
Chaſtity, it is to be held as
a point of faith, that this
gift will not be wanting
to any who will reſolue to

liue chaste, if he do as much
as lyeth in him to obteine
the same of Almignty God.

If there be so great difficulty to liue chaste in the
world, in so much that it
is not meritorious for a
man to bind himself therto
by vow; then such a vow is
of it owne nature vayne, &
of no effect to him that makes it, and so he may freely
breake that which is of
such difficulty, as seemes
morally impossible. But
this kind of reasoning may
by no meanes be admitted;
to wit, that such a vow is
                        of

of it owne nature vaine &
of no effect, and that it may
be broken without a most
grieuous sin. See the aboue
mentioned testimony of the
Apostle 1. *Tim.* 5.

It is very commenda-
ble & meritorious for yong
men also remayning in the
world to vow chastity, yea
the Church bindeth al such
as haue taken holy Orders
therunto. Therfore if men
do it, & that it be commendable in them to do so; why
should it not be the like for
women, such as are yonge,
both Maydes, & Widdows

G 3   especi-

especially, since men liue in
far greater danger by meanes
of their greater freedome
of conuersation, and their
lesse bashfullnes, togeather
with more frequent occasions of temptation. From
whence we see, it pro-
ceeds, that more men which
vow Chastity in the world
do offend against their vow
then women: yea there are
very few of that sexe who
vowing Chastity in the
world do violat their vow:
in so much that oftentimes
in a great citty, for the space
of many yeares, you shall
not

not hear of anyſuch:which
is a ſigne, that it is a matter
more eaſy for women to do
then for men ; & yet we ſee
that men do laudably take
vpon them ſuch vowes :
neither can they by any
meanes be excuſed frō thē,
being once vndertaken.

If it be meritorious to
keep Virginity in Religi-
on, why is it not alſo in the
World? For the circumſtan-
ce of the place alters not the
merit of the worke, but the
excellency it ſelfe thereof,
and a deuout will vnto it :
and this pious inclination

G 4   **may**

may be had as well out of
the state of Religion, when
a Virgin purposeth with
her selfe to abstaine from
Marriage, and to consecrate
her virginiry to Almighty
God, that she may serue him
the more perfectly, that she
may follow the counsell of
our Sauiour Christ, that she
may imitate our Lord, and
his most blessed Mother,
that she may apply all her
thoughts and affections to
heauenly things, and to the
health of her soule; for the
excellency of the worke is
equall on both sides. Therfore

fore there is no reason, why
the profession of Chastity
in the World, should not be
meritorious, as well as in
Religion.

It is not only commen-
dable in Monasteryes, but
also in the world, to do o-
ther good workes, as to
pray, to fast, to giue corporall and spirituall almes,
to chastice our body, and to
bind our selues by vow
thereunto. Then if other
good works loose not their
worth & esteem, nor their
merit before God by being
done in the world; why
should

ſhould Virginity, and ſingle
life ? Yea , as it is the more
prayſe-worthy to be tempe-
rate, and to abſtaine ſitting
at a banquet, and to be able
to bridle our appetite, euen
in the very middeſt of pro-
uocations ; ſo likewiſe may
it be a deed of greater merit
to liue chaſtly in the world,
where occaſions of falling
are more frequent : As for
example , when there are
lawfull reaſons why ſuch
occaſions might not be cō-
ueniently ſhunned , which
otherwiſe they would haue
willingly auoyded .

The

The state of being Religious, and to be shut vp in Monasteryes, is not agreeable with the complexion of euery one: yea a great many, either are not apt for this state, by reason of the weakenes of their body, or for other causes, or oftentymes their mindes are not easely wonne to it, and that most commonly for diuers sufficient reasons, which it is not necessary to reueale : and who now should cōstraine such to marry, or to enter into Monasteryes? Why should it not be lawfull

full for them to keepe their
virginity in the world, &
to vow themfelues vnto it?
Is it either becaufe they wil
not, nor cannot afcend to
the higheftdegree, that they
muft be therfore conftray-
ned to ftay in the loweft, &
may not keep a meane be-
t·vixt both? No man will
thinke fo, except he be indued with the fpirit of *Ioui-
uian.* The counfells and aduices of our Sauiour Chrift
are not fo neceffarely vnited one to the other, but
that one may be followed
without another, and by
them-

themselues, in diuers degrees. Wherfore as those who desire to obserue the state of Pouerty, are not bound vnto Chastity; so also those which imbrace Chastity, must not therfore of necessity keep Pouerty, or Obedience, or shut themselues vp in Monasteryes.

CHAP. V.

The same is proued out of the commodities which this state of life, being professed, both in the world and in Religion, doth bring with it.

THE Cause why this state of life is so commended

H

mended by holy Fathers,
as well in the one as the
other ; are the manifold
comodities which it brin-
geth therwith. For in both,
it is an imitation of An-
gelicall life;in both it is the
making of our body as it
were a burnt-offering to
Almighty God ; in both it
is a spirituall Marriage, in
which Christ is the spouse;
in both it freeth from the
irksome slauery of Marri-
age, and from the troubles
which belonge vnto it ;
in both it deliuereth the
minde from infinite cares
&

& troubles; finally in both it maketh it free, and at liberty to apply it selfe vnto God, and to dwel as it were mentally and spiritually with the Blessed, in community of heauenly things.

First it is an imitation of Angelicall life, as holy Fathers euery where do deliuer, out of the opinion of our Lord *Matt.* 22. Because as Angells marry not, nor are troubled with carnall concupiscence, but are euer attent to diuine matters, & entertaine themselues alwayes in them; so in like

H 2　　man-

manner Virgins are sayd to anticipate the glory of the Resurrection, because marriage after the Resurrection shall cease.

Virginity is a burnt-offering: for as in a burnt offring the thing sacrificed is killed, and afterward all of it consumed in the honour of God, that no part therof remaines for humaine vse: so likewise a Virgin must first kill all carnall affectiōs in her selfe, & afterwardes offer vp her body, mortified after this sort by the fire of Charity, to Almighty

mighty God, and reserue
no part thereof to any humaine or carnall vse.

She is a spirituall mar-
riage, because by vow she is
bound vnto God as to her
husband: for as the band of
carnall marriage is not to
be loosed ; neither also is
that of spirituall : yea that
of spirituall Marriage, is
much more indissoluble ;
for it cannot be loosed by
death it selfe, but continueth in all eternity. Againe,
as carnall marriage is effected for the mutuall enioy-
ing and comfort of both
    H 3   persons,

persons, and the bringing
forth of children : so this
Marriage is made, that the
soule may please God the
better, and receaue help &
comfort backe againe from
him, and that it may con-
uerse more familiarly , and
with the greater delight
with Almighty God , as
with its Spouse.

And finally, to the end
that hauing receaued seed
of diuine grace from him ,
an immortall and glorious
issue may be begotten to in-
herit in the world to come:
wherein spiritual Marriage

is

is farre more happy then
carnall; for the later is to
the end, that of impure and
corruptible seede, another
man may be begotten, and
that but to enioy a mortall
life, and thereby subiect to
infinite miseryes : but the
other is to the end, that out
of diuin seed a mortall man
should beget, not another
mortall man, but himselfe,
to an immortall and happy
life. Therefore he perswa-
deth himselfe first vnto this
marriage, and afterward by
word & example profiteth
others. To this may be lik-

H 4 wise

wife added, that as in carnall marriage, titles, and
dignityes, and all the goods
of either is communicated
to both: so likewife in fpirituall, the goods and dignityes of the efpoufed, belongeth alfo to the Spoufe.

The defire of a wife
is, that fhe may haue a huf-
band, who is faire, noble,
rich, powerfull, and cour-
teous, and if it happen that
fhe get fuch a one, fhe thinketh her felfe happy. But
how much more happy, is
a Virgin whofe husband is
the moft fayreft, moft noble,

ble, most rich, most powerfull, most gentle, and im-
mortal Lord of heauen and
earth, of Angells also, and
of men. See more of this in
S. *Ambrose* in his first booke
of Virgins.

For as much as belongs
to the benefits and commo-
dityes of holy Virginity,
they are generally three.
The first is, that it freeth
the mind from innumera-
ble troubles and afflictions
vnto which the state of matrimony either by meanes
of the wife or by meanes of
the childre is subiect vnto;
which

which the Apostle insinu-
ateth 1. *Cor.* 1. when he
speaketh in this manner of
those which are marryed :
*Tribulationem carnis habebunt
huiusmodi* ; such shal haue the
tribulation of the flesh.
And first of all, is the seruitude of the wife, by reason
that she hath not power of
her owne body, & is made
subiect in all thinges to her
husband, must endure his
frowardnes, his insolencies,
his banquetting, drukenes,
iealousy, suspicion, incontinency, adultery, taunts, &
blowes. Also she must follow

low him, sticke alwayes to him, obey him and serue him as his slaue ; so that many slaues in the world haue a more tollerable bō-dage, then some wiues vn-happily marryed; whilst he spends her wealth and sub-stance at dice, at play, in drinking, banquetting, pro-digall giuing, improfitable bargaines, improuident cō-tentions, and diuers other wayes, which his wife is not able to remedy.

Moreouer he leaueth the charge of prouiding for the whole house-hould to
                                her

her, and yet alloweth not wherwithall sufficiently to do it; and bringeth her oftentymes euen into that extremity, that she groweth halfe desperate. In the mean tyme being oppressed and ouercome with too much impatience, she often curseth her husband, and wisheth al il hap to befal him, and desireth nothing more then his death. Neither are these thinges rare and seldome, but the whole world is full of them.

Now if we should add vnto all this, the troubles that

that come continually by meanes of children, there would arise euen a whole world of miseryes & afflictions. And although in the carnall Act of marriage there seemeth to be now & then a little pleasure; yet of it owne nature, it is both vncleane (as a thing wherin we differ not fro a beast) and also full of shame and immodesty; & in a moment it is past, and afterward rewarded with innumerable discommodityes. For presently after Conception, there followeth a kind of

I   irke-

irkesomnes, idle dreames,
giddines, vnsetlednes of the
head, melancoly, conuulsi-
ons of the hart-stringes, ab-
surd longings after meates,
and a generall perturbation
of nature.

Then follow the paines
of child-bearing which are
both violent to the sense,
& oftentymes endure long,
and to many bring death
also; and then the Child being borne, with what great
care and solicitude must
it be brought vp, vntill it
come to be of some strength
and perfection of nature.
                          How

How many tymes a day
must it be made cleane,
fed, made vp, apparrelled,
laid to sleepe, rockt in the
cradell, taken out againe to
giue it suck, and be held
out. How many times must
it be flattered and intreated
with faire speaches & with
a thousand pretty hypocri-
sies and flatterings, to make
it leaue crying, or to sleepe?

These are the contynu-
all exercises of such as be
Mothers, and in such they
are imployed, not on ly all
day long, but also most part
of the night, so that they

I 2   can

can scarce take any rest but
with often interruption.

I omit the sluttishnes,
the ill sauour, the weeping,
crying, & brauling, which
they are constreyned dayly
to suffer. I omit allso the
cares and troubles, which
they haue when their children begin to grow big, &
to be exposed to diuers cha-
ces of the world. What
great greefe they haue, if it
chaunce they should mis-
carry and dye ; if by euil
company they should be al-
lured to villany and dishonesty ; if they should proue
stub-

stubborne and disobedient
against their Parents; if they
should spend & wast their
Parents goodes at play,
drinking, or at any other
vnlawful game; if without
their Parents consent they
should marry.

To these afflictions the
whole life of all such as are
mothers, is always subiect;
for albeit the Parents be
very deuout and religious,
yet it happens oftentymes
that the children bewicked
and lewd, and with their
misdemeanours, and ill liuing, torment their Parēts,

I 3   as

as wee haue examples in
Adam and *Cain*, in *Noë* and
Cham, in *Abraham* and *Ismael*,
in *Isaac* and *Esau*, in *Iacob*
and many of his sonnes, in
Dauid, *Amon*, and *Absolom*,
with infinite others: therfore since sacred virginity
deliuers from all this, it is
deseruedly to be numbred
amongst the greatest bene-
fitts that are.

Another commodity of
virginity and single life is,
that it freeth the minde frō
all cares of gouerning a family, of increasing the
stocke and wealth of their
estate

estate, of marrying their children, & of leauing them ample Patrimonyes ; for of these foure things all Parents are for the most part most careful & sollicitous; yea commöly their minds are so wholly addicted and giuen to such businesses, as they can scarce euer thinke seriously on God, or things belonging to the good of their soule.

These things they keep alwayes in minde, in these things they spend all their thoughts and affections, these things so waste and
I 4   weare

weare out all the ability &
powers of their mindes, as
they haue no ftrength left
to confider, or thinke vpon
things that are eternall.

Greatly therfore is the
mifery of this eftate to be
pittyed; for the bondage of
the mynd is more hurtfull
a great deale, then that of
the body; and the loffe of
good thoughts, is a greater
domage, then the loffe of
money.

The third cōmodity of
virginity and fingle life is,
that it maketh the minde,
being freed from the cares
                        and

and troubles of Marriage,
more fit & prepared to serue
Almighty God, and pro-
cure its owne safety: and
this is the greatest good of
this life. For which cause it
is commended specially by
the Apostle the 1. *Cor. 7.*
where he saith, *Mulier innup-*
ta &c. A womā vnmarryed,
and a Virgin thinketh on
what belongeth vnto God,
that she may be holy, both
in body and minde.

There is nothing better
nor more healthfull vnto
our soule thē to serue God,
and to endeauour the ob-
tayning

teyning of our foules well-
fare. To this purpofe were
we made, & adorned with
thefe noble faculties of our
foule, Vnderftanding, Me-
mory, and Will. Wee haue
not recciuedthefeto imploy
them about tranfitory and
feruile matters, without a-
ny fruit at al, but to addreffe
them to eternall and celefti-
all things, for our great be-
nifit and aduantage. All
earthly things are to bafe &
cōtemptible for our minds
(which is aboue all vifible
things) to fixe, and exercife
it felfe there about. The
                    fhortnes

shortnes it selfe of our life,
togeather with the vncer-
tinry & necessity of dying,
might iustly recall vs from
the care of temporall matters, & addresse our thoghts
to the solicitude of thinges
eternall . Whereupon the
Apostle 1 . *Cor. 7.* sayth : *Tē-*
pus breue est &c. Time is short,
it remaines , that such as
haue wiues, be as those who
haue them not ; and those
who mourne, like those
who mourne not; & those
who reioyce, like those
who reioyce not; and those
who buy, like those who
posseste

posseſſe not; and thoſe who
vſe this world, like thoſe
who vſe it not ; for the fa-
ſhion of this world paſſeth
away &c.

By which wordes he
teacheth vs, that we ſhould
be no more affected and addicted to tranſitory things,
then as if they did not belong vnto vs. We ought to
haue care of nothing ſo
much, as to auoyd eternall
puniſhment , and attaine
to euerlaſting ioyes : for in
compariſon of theſe, all the
good or ill of this world,
ought to be of no account :
                          So

So that if there were nothing but madnes practised in the world, this would be the greatest, to neglect the highest and euerlasting thinges, & to follow that which is base and transitory, with so great hazard of eternall damnation.

Therfore as that manner of life is miserable, and to be auoyded by all wise men, which intangleth the mind with care of base & earthly thinges, howsoeuer glorious and honourable they seeme: So on the contrary, is that state happy &

K   most

most desirously to be imbraced, which freeth the mind from all these cares & troubles, and affoardeth it commodity to meditate on heauenly things, and to apply it selfe to the obtayning of its own welfare. And such is single life, as it hath byn shewed.

Neither in women only, but also in men single life hath all these effectes: for most of those thinges which we haue sayd before of women, haue place also in men: yet men in Marriage are most commonly ex-posed

posed to more discommo-
dityes and inconueniences
then women , because the
whole care of maintayning
the houshould , and of the
greatest busines lyeth vpon
him; and infinite disdaines
of the wife , offences , iea-
losies, suspicions, côplaints,
and frowardnes are to be
endured, as *S. Hierome* pro-
secuteth it , very elegantly
out of *Theophrastus* the Phi-
losopher in his first booke
against *Iouinianus* , whose
words it seemeth heer good
to set downe.

Fertur, inquit, Aureolus &c.

Heere

Heer is brought (quoth he)
a litle goulden booke of
Theophraſtus written concerning marriage, in which
he asketh this queſtion,
Whether a wiſe man ſhould
marry a wife or no? And
when he hath defined, that
if ſhe were fair, wel broght
vp, of good Parents, and if
ſhe were healthfull & rich,
with theſe conditions a
wiſe man might ſomtimes
marry; he preſently infer-
reth: But all theſe ſeldome
match togeather in marriage, therfore it is not behoo-
full for a wiſe man to mar-

ry

ry. &c . And then he fets
downdiuersreafons which
the fame Philofopher alledg-
geth for his opinion.

Firft (quoth he) it
hinders the ftudy of Philo-
fophy; for no man can ferue
his bookes and his wife at
once . There are alfo many
thinges which are neceffary
for the vfe of Wiues , as
gay apparell gold, Iewells
expenfes, wayting women,
variety of houfholdftuffe ,
guilded horfe-litters , and
coaches. Moreouer you fhal
haue all the night long nothing but pratling, & com-
K 3   plaintes

plaintes that this Dame
weares better cloaths when
she goes abroad then she:
This Lady, or Gentlewo-
man is much honoured and
respected of all whersoe-
uer she comes; whilest I,
poore soule, am despised &
contemned of euery body.
Why did you looke so ear-
nestly on my Neighbours
wife? Why did you talke
with her mayd? Are you
come frō the Market, what
haue yee bought? &c.

Her husband cannot haue
a friend or companiō, but
straight she thinketh that
the

the loue of another is her
hatred. If there were a learned Maister in euery town,
men should neither forsake
their wiues, nor be able to
walke with so great a burthen. If she be poore, it is
cost to help her, if rich, a
torment to endure her.

Moreouer there is no
choice of a wife, but what
a one soeuer you chance
to take, if she be colerique,
if a foole, if deformed, if
proud, if sluttish, what fault
soeuer she hath, we learne
that afterward. A Horse,
an Asse, an Oxe, a Dog, the

K 4   worst

worst slaue a man can en-
tertaine ; his apparell also,
his kettles, his chayres, his
cups, his earthen pots, all
these a man may proue be-
fore he buy them, only his
wife must not be shewed
before she be had, for feare a
man should so dislike her,
that he would neuer haue
her.

You must alwayes be
looking on her face, and
commending her beauty,
for feare least if you looke
on another, she thinke that
her beauty displeaseth you.
She must be called Mistresse
and

and her Birth-day must be
made a Holy day: you must
sweare by her health, and
you must pray that she may
out liue you : you must re-
uerence her that nurst her,
and her also that bare her
when she was a little one,
her seruant, her brother-in-
law, her little dandling,
her pretty Page, her hyred
Prooür, and her Eunuch
forsooth, for the longer con-
tinuance and more security
of lust (vnder all which
names are prettily couched
Adulterers.) And whome-
soeuer of all these she affe &-
&eth,

&teth, he must be beloued
too, euen bythose to whom
they are vngratefull.

If you commit the go-
uernement of the whole
house to her charge, you
must be her seruant . If you
reserue any part of it to
your selfe , she thinks you
wil not trust her, & straight
turneth into hatred, and
scoulding , and vnles you
beware of her betymes, you
are in danger to be poyso-
ned .

Old women , Wisards,
brokers of Iewels and silke
apparel, if you admit any of
these

these into your house, you
are in dáger of cuckolding:
and if you forbid them,
you do her wronge to sul-
pect her.

But to what end is it
to watch her narrowly,
when a wife that is vnchast
can neuer be restrained : &
if she be chast, she ought not
to be restayned; for the con-
straint of chastity is but an
vnfaythfull keeper. She only is truly to be named chast
who can be otherwise if she
wil. A faire wife is a bay te,
aswell in other mens eyes,
as in his that hath her. A
slut

flut wil fooner defire others
then they her . It is a hard
matter to enioy that alone
which many men feeke af-
ter; and it would be a trouble to haue fuch a one, as
no body would vouchfafe
to affect. Yet it is a leffe mifery to haue an ill fauoured
wife, then to keepe a faire
one true. There is nothing
fafely poffeft by one, which
of euery body is wifht for.

One follicits with his
comlynes, another with his
wit, another with his plea-
fantnes, another with his
money: by fome meanes or
　　　　　　　　　other

other at laſt the Fort will be
taken, which is on euery
ſide ſo ſtrongely beſeiged.

But it may be obiected,
that it is neceſſary for a mā
to haue a wife, to take
charge of the expéſes of his
howſe, or to be a comfort
to him when he languiſ-
ſheth, or to auoyd ſolitary-
nes. To this I anſwere, that
a faithfull ſeruant obeying
the authority of his maiſter,
and doing his buſines ac-
cording to his will, diſpo-
ſeth of matters a great deale
better then a wife, who
thinketh that her Miſtres-
L ſhip

ship cõfitteth in doing that
which is againft her huf-
bands will, that is to fay,
to do that which fhe hath a
will to, not that which fhe
is commaunded to do.

And as for attending &
comforting a man when he
is ficke, his friends and fer-
uants, or fuch poore foules
as he hath made beholding
vnto him, may better do it
then fhe, who vpbraides
him, as it were, with the
teares which fhee fheedes
for him, yea fells the very
filth and droffe therof, in
hope to be his executour.
                    And

And by this boasting of her carefullnes, neuer leaues him, til with her perpetual trouble, she driues him into vtter desperation.

But if her finger chance to ake, he must be sicke for it, and neuer budge from her bed side. Or if she be a good wife, and of a sweete disposition (which notwithstanding is a rare bird) he must groane with her, whilst she is in child bed, & he payned with her danger.

As for the auoyding of solitarines, a wise man can

L 2   neuer

neuer be alone: he hath present all those which are,
or euer were good, in his
thoughts, & freely placeth
his mind on what he will.
That which he cannot do
with his body, he imbra-
ceth with his thoughts, &
if there be sarcity of men to
conuerse withal, he talketh
with God; he is neuer lesse
alone then when he wants
all company.

Besides it is a most idle
thing to take a wife, in regard to haue children by
her that his family may not
be extinct, or that he haue,
                    help

help & ayde in his old age, and also to know who shall in herit that which he leaues behind. For what is one the better when he is going out of the world, that another is called by his name, when as a sonne can not presently be like his Father; and there are an infinite number of other men also perhaps called by the same name. Or what booteth it to nourish those at hom, who we hope may be helps to vs whē we are old, whē perhaps they either dy before vs, or become of such

L 3   a

a peruerfe difpofition, as
they will not fuccour vs; or
if they themfelues come to
maturity of yeares, perhaps
they thinke their parents
liue to longe.

And as for heires , our
friends & our neighbours
whom we loue, are better &
more fure heyres vnto vs,
being chofen thereunto by
vs freely, the thofe whome
wee are conftreyned to
haue whether we will or
no: though indeed it be a
for more affured inheritan-
ce to make our felues our
owne heires , (by doyng
good

good workes whilst we
liue, (for otherwise we do
but abuse the same) then to
leaue it, being gotten all
by our owne industry and
pains, to the vncertein vses
of any others whatsoeuer.

These reasons and the
like *Theophrastus* discussing,
what good Christiã might
he not make ashamed of
such vanities and troubles,
whose conuersation ought
to be in heauen, and who
dayly sayth *Cupio dissolui &c.*
I desire to be dissolued and
be with Christ: as though
he who may be a coheyre

with

with Christ himself, should
desire to haue man to be
his heire, and should wish
for children, and be deligh-
hted in the succession of
his posterity whome per-
haps Antichrist shall per-
uert ; when notwithstan-
ding wee read that *Moyses*,
and *Samuel* preferred others
before their own children.
Neither yet did they ac-
count the children whome
they sawe displease Almi-
ghty God.

Thus farre are S. *Hiero-*
mes words, who afterward
confirmeth the same with
exam-

examples out of the old
Testament. By which it is
manifestly shewed how far
single life in the world is to
be preferred aboue Marriage, and out of how many
discommodityes & cares it
doth deliuer a man; and
what aboundance of helpe
it affoardeth to a man, to
passe ouer pleasantly, and
quietly this temporall life,
and obteine a high degre in
the euerlasting. All which
things if they should be
exactly weighed and con-
sidered of most men, I doubt
not, but there would be
farre

farre fewer who would fo
much admire, loue, and
imbrace the feruitude, that
Marryage oftentimes brin-
geth with it.

CHAP. VI.

Of the Merits of both States of life, to wit, of vnmarried and married.

SOME one will obiect,
That if the paines and
troubls of mothers be great
in bearing and breeding
their children, and in fup-
porting the conditions and
iniuryes of their husbands;
great alfo are the merits of
endu-

enduring them : which
merits such as are virgins
cannot haue . Whence the
Apostle also 1. *Tim* 2. saith:
Saluabitur &c. She shall be
saued , by bringing forth
children &c .

I answere , that Parents
may be moued with a dou-
ble affection , to beget and
bring vp children : to wit ,
with a meere humaine and
naturall affection , & . with
a spirituall or diuine. A naturall affection is , when
any one desireth children
for the conseruation of his
name & family that he may
haue

haue heires to whome he
may leaue his goods; that
he may out-liue his owne
death in his posterity ; that
he may be honoured in thē;
that he may haue comfort
and help by his children.
All these are humaine res-
pects and affections , and
therfore of no merit , or esteeme before God ; yet of
their owne nature they are
not ill , but indifferent.
Wherfore those who out of
such affection do contract
Marriage, or beget childrē,
or bring them vp begotten,
merit nothing before Al-
mighty

mighty God, and loose all
their labours and charges
which they are at, as far
forth as this; to wit, that
they shall not receiue eternall reward for them, but
onely a temporall comfort
or comodity. For as an humaine affection is not meritorious before Almighty
God, no more also is the
work which followeth out
of it, although it be frequét
and laborious.

In like manner to loue
and follow Honours, Ri-
ches, Magistracy, Dignit-
tyes and Pleasures for the

M   com-

commodity, splendor and
sweetnes which we per-
ceiue in them, although of
it selfe it be no sinne; neither likewise is it of any de-
sert, but rather apperteineth
to the delight of such things
as are the concupiscence of
the flesh, of the eyes, and
pride of life, and which pro-
cede out of a corrupt nature, not out of the inspiratiō
of diuine grace.

The same likewise is
to be sayd of the affections
of Parents, whereby they
wish and procure these cō-
sents & pleasures vnto their
chil-

children. For euen as whé
they desire and obtayne
these things for themselues,
they deserue nothing at the
handes of Almighty God;
no more likewise doe they
when they doe the like in
their childrens behalfe: yea
this affection is not onely
not meritorious before Almighty God, but also it is
not so much as a worke of
any vertue.

For first of all, that it
not a worke proceeding
out of any diuine or infused
vertue, it is manifest, since
it may be foud also in Hea-
M 2   thens

thens themselues, and the
moſt wicked perſons that
liue. Alſo that ſuch affections proceed not out of any
morall or Philoſophicall
vertue it is plaine, for they
reſpect not their obiects,
as they are honeſt and rea-
ſonable, as the natures of
ſuch vertues require, but as
they are delightfull & cō-
modious, or honourable.

Whence it is, that no man
by ſuch an affection becommeth praiſeworthy, which
is the propriety of vertue.
As no man is worthy of
prayſe, for that he loueth or
geteth

getteth riches, honors, plea-
fures, or for louing his child
becaufe he is fair, or becaufe
he is like him, for finging
wel, dancing wel, fpeaking
well, or being indewed
with fuch like ciuill ornaments or qualityes. Al fuch
affections are only naturall
and indifferent, and therefore of no defert or merit in
the fight of Almighty God
before his Tribunall feate.

Therfore as he which
giueth almes to the poore
prodigally, and vayneglo-
rioufly to make himfelf honoured and efteemed the

M 3   more

more of men, according to
the wordes of our Sauiour,
ſhal haue no reward before
Almighty God, but recea-
ueth all his reward in the
prayſes which he getteth of
men in ſo doing : So thoſe,
which marry for reſpect of
pleaſure or riches, thoſe
which deſire to haue children, or to bring them vp
to haue contentment, who
day and night onely take
care, how they may leaue
them a large and ample in-
heritance, that they may
promote them to honours,
offices, dignityes, or weal-
                        thy

thy marriages, deserue nothing before God, but re-
ceaue their reward in the
temporall contentements,
which by this meanes they
procure, either to themselues, or to their children.

Therefore to speake
truely, their labours and
cares are all lost; neither do
they reape any fruit at all
to be accounted of from all
this; for nothing is to be e-
steemed of any great valew,
but that which is euerla-
sting.

All temporall things
are of small account, passing

away

away as shaddows, & ther-
fore most vnworthy to
spend al the vigour & principal acts of our soule about
thē, which were ordained
for things eternal. Heerupō
holy Scripture euery where
calleth vs from the loue and
desire of riches, honours,
and pleasures, and telleth
vs that such as are poore,
meeke & oppressed, are only happy.

Neither are all these la-
bours and paines of Parents
onely vnprofitable, but they
are also hurtfull, and the
originall cause of infinite
euils

euils. From hence it is, that
there are such an infinite
nūber of men in the world,
who damne there owne
soules (which otherwise
might haue been saued) for
their childrens sake, to mak
them rich , or to promote
them to Honours. For those
that wil become rich as the
Apostle witnesseth, *fall into*
temptation, and the snare of the
deuill, and into many vnprofitable
and hurtfull desires, which send
them head long into damnatiō , &
destruction; for couetous desire is
the roote of all mischeife.

Marriage doth comonly
force

force men headlong vnto
this desire, for al mē would
make their children rich, &
leaue them a large inheri-
tance ; so that deseruedly
also for that cause, that state
of life is not to be greatly
desired, which maketh all
our paines and cares, most
commonly, not only vn-
profitable for our welfare,
but also dangerous and
hurtfull vnto vs, if it be not
auoyded . Yet it followes
not from hence, that wed-
locke is euill: for neither
Riches or Honnors be euil
but good, which God also
　　　　　　　　　some-

sometymes bestoweth vpō
vs, for the reward of some
good deed or other ; and in
tymes past haue beene pro-
mised also to those few
who obserued the law : but
it is dangerous I say, to loue
such pleasures and delights,
to follow them, and to imploy al our endeauors onely
in attayning of them, since
they are but base & meane,
and do hinder the loue and
desire of things eternall, &
intágle the minde in many
snares.

In like manner, though
Matrimony of it selfe be
good,

good , and ordeyned by
God , yet it drawes with it
many cares and troubles ,
which through humanie
frailty hinder the health
of the soule, that it leades
men secretly into many
sins , and oftentimes vnto
eternall damnation. Thus
much of the humaine af-
fectiō ,out of which many
men inclyne vnto Marry-
age .

The spirituall affection
is , when Parents desire to
haue children , to the end
that they may instruct them
in the feare of God , that
                    they

they may teach them to
serue him , that they may
increase the number of the
faithful, that by them many
deeds of deuotion may be
done , that God may be ho-
nored by them and the like:
these affections rise not
out of nature; but out of di-
u ne inspiration , and are
worthy of a man, as he is a
Christian.

Whence I confesse that
Parents who with this kind
of affection desire to haue
yssue , and bring them vp,
as aforsaid , do merit greatly before Almighty God;

N   and

& the wife alſo who with
ſuch a ſpirit deſireth Marriage, ſhalbe ſaued by the
bearing of children. And
in this manner the wordes
of the Apoſtle are to be vn-
derſtood 1. *Tim*. 2. But yet
it ſeemes to be more probable, that the Apoſtle in that
place ſpeaketh not of the
merit, but of the eſtate and
office of Marriage; & that to
be alſo the meaning of this
ſaying, *Saluabitur &c.* She
ſhalbe ſaued, by doing the
office of Marryage, and en-
deauouring to haue chil-
dren: for ſo the Greeke text
doth

doth import, as the learned
do teach.

So likewise to the Ro-
mans *cap.* 4. 5. *&* 11. *Abrahā*
is sayd to be the Father of
those that belieue, by hauing
the foreskin or Prepuce cut
off, that is to say, by those
which are in that Estate.
And in 2. *Cor. cap.* 6. *Per*
gloriam & ignobilitatem &c. By
glory and ignobility, by in-
famy and good credit, that
is to say, in prosperity and
aduersity. The same is confirmed by the words which
the Apostle addeth, *Saluabi-*
tur &c. She shalbe saued (saith
N 2   he)

he) by the bearing of childrē, if she perseuere in faith,
in loue, & in holynes, with
sobriety: therefore he attri-
buteth the cause of saluati-
to fayth, & to loue &c. not
to the precreation of children: yet I confesse also that
this very deed is meritorious likewise, if it be done,
as we haue sayd, out of
spirituall affection: but it is
otherwise, if it be done out
of humaine only.

Moreouer, if this estate
and the offices thereof, be
chosen & performed with
a spirituall affection : neuertheles

uertheles single life is much better and more meritorious; both because it remoues innumerable occasions of distractions, imperfections, and sinnes, by which the estate of Matrimony is hindred in the offices of deuotion; and also because it affoardeth comodity of conuersing dayly with God and of being attent to diuin matters. Waerefore a Virgin oftentymes may merit more in one day, then a marryed woman in many monethes.

N 3   CHAP.

CHAP. VII.

*Of certaine thinges to be obserued
in this Estate.*

TO the end that Vir-
gins may the better
preserue this treasure, & obtayne their scope and purpose more at larg, by which
they haue so straitly bound
themselues vnto God, and
vndertaken this estate; holy Fathers haue prescribed
certaine things to be obserued. First in their apparell;
secondly in their exercises;
thidly in the vse of their riches and wealth; & lastly
in

in their conuerſation.

As for their apparell,
it muſt not be coſtly, but
decent and graue, without
any kind of vanity or curi-
oſity, without pride alſo, or
any ſecular ornaments, ſuch
as may repreſent the ſtate
wherein they liue, and the
forſaking of the world; by
which euery man that ſees
them, may know that they
are Virgins, and haue an
intent neuer to marry. For
by this meanes they ſhall a-
uoyd all importunityes and
troubles, which ſuiters are
accuſtomed to vſe: and be-

N 4   ſides

sides this they shall preuent
many other inticements to
the breach of their intent.

S. *Cyprian* in his booke
de disciplina & habitu Virginum,
handieth this place more at
large, and with great ele-
gancy : Continency (quoth
he) & Chastity consist not
only in the integrity of the
body, but also in the honor
of the Attire and apparell,
being ioyned with mode-
sty. She must not only be a
Virgin really, but also she
must be knowne, and be
belieued to be such a one :
so that no man who seeth
her

her who is a Virgin, may
haue any doubt whether
she be so or no. For why
should she go adorned, or
attyred as though she had,
or would haue a husband?
let her rather feare to please
any, if she be a Virgin; neither let her seeke her owne
danger, since she preserues
her selfe for a better & more
deuout purpose &c. Nei-
ther ought a Virgin to be
delighted with the shew of
her owne beauty, or to take
a glory in her owne person
or comlynes, since she hath
no resistance or war against
any

any thing, so much, as a-
gainst the flesh, nor any
more obstinate enemy to o-
uercom the her own body.

Afterwards he alleadg-
eth some, who excuse the-
selues for their Riches and
Nobility, for which res-
pects they thinke that it is
conuenient for them to go
more richly attyred; whose
excuse he refuteth at large,
shewing in what thinges
they should imploy their
wealth.

To their habit also be-
longeth a Veyle, with the
which it is meete that a
Virgin

Virgin should be couered
when she goeth abroad,
least either she might see
that which were not befit-
ting, or her countenance
should be perceaued of o-
thers. For how many, I
pray you, haue there beene
in the world, who only by
sight haue either perished
themselues, or killed others?
In so much that they must
take principal heed of their
eyes. And *Tertullian* hath
written a particuler Trea-
tise vpō this subiect of virgins veyling and couering
their heads, which he iudged

ged to be a thing so necessary, that he sayd: It was no
lesse then a passion of lust,
to a vertuous Virgin, euery
tyme that she exposeth her
selfe to publique view; to
wit, because that therby she
with her face open, casting
her eyes freely about to see,
& to be seene, is easily cor-
rupted in spirit; & that the
very gazing it self is a signe
of an vnchast mind.

And againe afterward:
The desire not to be veyled
or couered is not a chast desire, but admiteth somwhat
that belongeth not vnto a
Vir-

Virgin; as also the desire to
delight others in beholding
her; for true, entyre, and
pure Virginity feareth nothing so much, as it owne
selfe, yea it endureth not the
eyes of other women that
delight in gazing, since the
eyes of it selfe are farre dif-
ferent from such; it flyeth
to the veyle of her head, as
to a helmet, & as to a buck-
ler which defendeth her; it
is a protection against the
blowes of temptation, a-
gainst the darts of scandals,
against suspitions, & whis-
pering, and emulation, yea
    O   and

and against Enuy it felfe.
After this put on the armor
of bafhfullnes, entrench thy
felfe within the bullwarke
of modefty, build vp a wall
for thy fex, which keepeth
in thyne own eyes, and let-
teth not the eyes of others
to enter. Thou baft marryed Chrift and deliuered thy
body to him, thou haft efpoufed the maturity of thy
yeares to him. Goe accor-
ding to his will and pleafure; it is Chrift that bid-
deth thofe who are marry-
ed to others, to veile themfelues, much more thofe
                    which

which are espoused vnto
him.

For this purpose the
womens attyres of *Brabant*
are very fit, which are called by them *Huekes*, which
the very noblest Matrons
of that Country vse, when
they would not be knowne
in any publike assembly.

Let vs now come to the
exercises which holy Fa-
thers prescribe to be vsed
by virgins. These are fasting, prayer, reading of spirituall bookes, and handy-
worke, in the dayly vse and
variety wherof they may

spend all their tyme most
profitably.

Fasting is as it were the
foundation & ground of al
other vertues ; for by this
the roote of many tempta-
tions, and by consequence
of many vices, is cut of;the
minde is made more fit to
conuerse dayly with Almi-
ghty God, with great com-
fort & fruit,from whome
it conceiueth all its good,
frōwhence al Saints for the
most part haue deriued the
begining of a spiritual life.
By fasting,I meane not such
fasting, as should weaken
or

or impaire nature: but such wherby the body becomes more healthfull, the mind more quicke, and the concupiscence more subiect.

S. *Hierome* commendeth greatly this exercise in his 8. Epistle to *Demetriades*, *de cuftodia virginit*. Atter (saith he) diligent taking heed of impure thoughts, you must put on the ornament of fasting, and sing with *Dauid*, I haue humbled my soule in fasting, &c. And then afterwardes. Fasting is not a perfect vertue of it selfe, but the foundation of

O 3   others

others, and is both sanctifi-
fication & chastity, without which no man shall
euer see God. It affoardeth
staires to such as wil ascend
to the top; & yet if it should
be alone, it is not sufficient to crowne a virgins &c.

In which words it is to
be noted, that fasting is tearmed by *S. Hierome*, Sanctification, and Chastity of o-
ther vertues. It is called
Sanctification, because it
maketh others vertues flo-
rish, and works their effects
the better; and by this meanes it sanctifieth.

It

It is called Chaſtity , becauſe it procureth cleaneſſe
of body and hart , wherin
conſiſt all other vertues ,
without which no man
ſhall ſee God .

And that this faſting muſt
be moderate, & ſuch as may
not weaken the body , but
refreſh & quické the mind ,
S. *Ierome* warneth vs in theſe
words, when he ſaith: Neither do I preſcribe to yow
immoderate faſting, or ſuch
abſtinences , as ſhould be
altogether without meat,
by which bodyes that are
tender and delicate may be

O 4   quickly

quickly brought out of health, and grow sicke, be-
fore they haue layde the
foundation of this holy
conuerſation .

S.Ambroſe in his firſt book
of virgins ſaith , that the
ſparing of meate , and ab-
ſtinence from drinke , maketh a man to be ignorant
of vice ; for it maketh him
to be ignorant of the cauſes
therof . Therfore let this be
rather a faſt of ſobriety thē
affliction .

Prayer alſo, vnder which
is conteyned the meditatiō
of heauenly things, and the
                    myſteries

mysteries of our faith, is
principally necessary. First,
because by this wee must
obteyne dayly supply of
Grace, wherby we may
both resist temptations and
fulfill Gods diuine Com-
mandements, and perseue-
re to the end: wherfore our
Lord warneth vs, that we
alwayes pray, to wit, as
much as conueniently we
may, and as far forth as the
fraylty, and necessary affai-
res of this world will permit vs: for our perseueran-
ce and eternall safety de-
pendeth on Prayer.

Secon-

Secondly by Prayer &
Meditation we lift vp out
mynd to Almighty God ,
we place our selues in his
sight and presence; wee cõ-
sider his maiesty, his Power,
and his Wisedome , his
Goodnes & his prouidence,
his Mercy and his Iustice ;
we adore him , and praise
him , we giue him thankes
and blesse him ; there we
deale with him about the
busines of our Saluation ,
and call to mynd all things
which he hath both done
and suffered for vs.

For this cause especially,
a Vir-

a Virgin must abandone
Marriage and secularity, &
imbrace the state of holy
Virginity , according to
the Apostole , to wit , that
she may thinke of these
things which belonge to
our Lord , that she may be
holy in body and spirit, that
she may behaue her selfe
worthily in the presence &
conuersation of Almighty
God, that she may sticke so
close vnto him., that she
may neuer be drawn away:
and as our Interpreter tran-
flateth it, that she may haue
free leaue to beseech any
thing

thing of our Lord, without
hinderance.

Heere are delights and
spirituall comforts; in this
consisteth as it were the Pa-
radise of our soules; by these
things our conuersation is
in heauen, and we are made
to enioy the society of Angels: without these what-
soeuer we do, is dry & barren, for all comfort and spirituall ioy proceedeth from
the attentiue consideration
of diuine matters.

From whence it com-
meth, that those who apply
not themselues with great
loue

loue and defire, to Prayer
and Meditation, they muft
needs remaine dry, or at
leaftwife they fhall neuer
taft the moft excellent delights of the fpirit. By Prayer & meditation the mind
is exercyfed, and groweth
zealous in the function &
habit of other vertues, becaufe the guift of grace is
more aboundantly obtey-
ned by it, whereby the labour of vertue is made more
eafy and delightfull.

Hence the Royall Pro-
phet faith, *Viam mādatorū &c.*
I haue runne the courfe and
P   way

way of thy commaunde-
ments , whilst thou dila-
tedst my hart with ioy. And
why ? becaufe the vanity
of the world, & the worth
of vertue , and the Charity
of God, and the reward of
life to come , are shewed
therby vnto vs . The confi-
deration of all which, must
needs greatly stir vs vp to
all offices of vertue, and to a
diligent care of our owne
faluation .

Reading of Spirituall
bookes alfo is commended
by the holy Fathers , and
commeth very neere to the
exercife

exerciſe of Prayer. For as by Prayer we obteyne the conuerſation euen of God himſelfe ; ſo do we it alſo by reading of ſpirituall books. Whereupon *Iſidorus* in his 3.booke of Sentences the 8. *Chap*. ſaith : Who alwayes wil conuerſe with God, muſt pray often, and read much ; for when we pray, we ſpeake familiarly vnto God, but when we read, he ſpeaketh vnto vs.

And afterward he addeth, that Spirituall profit alſo proceedeth from praying and reading.

P 2   Laſtly

Lastly handy-worke is greatly comméded, for this is an especiall and beneficiall Exercise for three things. The first is, therby somewhat to release and refresh our minde ; for we cannot alwayes attend to read or pray , but it is needfull to recreate our minde by intermixing of labours sometymes betwée, least we should be ouerwearyed : and this is done most conueniently by outward imployments , in which the mind is little or nothing at all buyfied.

Whence

Whence it followeth,
that this manner of variety
becommeth most gratefull
to our weake and changea-
ble Nature, and hath beene
vsed in all ages by men and
women, such as were holy;
and likewise it helpeth to
auoyd idlenes, which is especially to be taken heed
of, by all such as endeauour
to attaine to the perfection
of a deuout and holy life.
For as *S. Ierome* in his Epistle
to *Demetriades* sayth, there
is nothing more hurtfull to
any deuout purpose then
Idlenes, which doth not

P 3   onely

only omit to get new perfectió, but also wasteth that which was gotten before. And Blessed *Ignatius* saith, *Otium omnium malorum &c.* Idlenes is said to be the beginning of all mischiefe ; for a minde that is not imployed, is open to all suggestions and impressions of the diuell.

Wherby sometymes it commeth to passe , as *Seneca* witnesseth, that although the body be guiltlesse, yet the mind being idle, falleth into a thousande sorts of lewdnesse. Wherfore it is
good

good to be alwaies doing
of somewhat, and to im-
ploy our minds about one
good action or other, that
the diuell may alwayes find
vs busy.

Lastly it is beneficiall
for the health of our body,
and to giue good example
also, and to releeue others.
For no Almes is so pleasing
to Almighty God, no guift
so acceptable, as that which
is earned by our owne la-
bours. S. *Hierom* discourseth
at large of this point in his
epistle to *Demetriades*, which
for breuities sake I omit.

It

It resteth now to speake
of the third, to wit of the
vse of their Riches. Holy
Fathers set downe the manner at large, how amongst
Virgins, those who are
wealthy shold imploy their
meanes; to wit, not in superfluous apparell, not in
banquetting and pleasures,
not in adorning their bo-
dyes, not in Iewels, pearles,
rings, bracelets, not in rich
& curious houshould-stuff,
not in riot and excesse of
brauery aboue their neighbours; but in the succour &
releife of the poore, and of
                      such

such as are seruants of God.

S. *Cyprian* in his booke
De disciplina & habitu Virginum,
discourseth at large vpon
this thing: I will only al-
leadge one sentence for breu-
ityes sake: *Locupletem te dicis
&c.* Thou boastest (quoth
he) that thou art wealthy
and rich, and thou thinkest
that it behooueth thee to
vse the riches which God
hath permitted thee to pos-
sesse. Do so, vse them, but
let it be in such thinges as
may concerne the health of
thy soule. Vse them, but in
that which God hath com-
maun-

maunded thee to vſe them,
& in which he hath ſhew-
ed thee & taught thee how
to doe . Let the poore find
thee to be rich, and thoſe
that are needy perceaue thee
to be wealthy . Put out thy
Patrimony to vſe , into the
handes of Almighty God.
Giue meate vnto Chriſt,
that it may be lawfull for
thee to ſuſtayne the glory of
thy Virginity . And to the
end that it may be rewar-
ded by our Lord , beg it of
him by the prayers of ma-
ny. Lay vp thy treaſures
there, where no thiefe can
                        dig

dig them out, where no wait-layer, or night-robber can breake through. Purchase to thy selfe possessions, but let them be of heauen, where neither rust shall eate, nor hayle fall vpon, nor Sunne burne, nor rayne corrupt thy fruites, they being continuall and euerlasting, free from the touch of secular abuse &c.

And *S. Hierome* in his Epistle to *Demetriades* sayth: *Consideremus &c.* Let vs consider how wisely Wisdome it self hath spoken: *Sell what thou hast.* To whome is this commanded

commanded? To wit, to
him to whome it is fayd:
If thou wilt be perfect, fell
not a part of thy goods, but
all. And when thou haft
fould them, what follow-
eth? Giue them to the poor,
not to the rich, not to thy
Neighbors who are weal-
thy, not to maintaine ex-
ceffe, but to fuffice neceffity.
Whether he be a Prieft, or
thy cozen, or kinfman, thou
fhalt confider in him no o-
ther refpect but his pouerty.
Let the bowels of thofe that
are hungry, not the fat banquets of thofe that furfet receaue

ceaue thy almes &c.

Yet for all this it is not the meaning of S. *Hierom*, that if a Virgin entreth not into Religiõ, she should depriue her selfe, of that which is needfull for her selfe to liue on in good sor; but that she bestow thereit which she hath superfluous, for the vse of the poore, & that after the manner which she iudgeth to be most to the honour of God.

S. *Cyprian* before mentioned goeth yet forward, speaking to those who hauing vowed Virginity, and are

Q   very

very rich & wealthy, thus:
But there be some rich women & very wealthy, who
will set out, and shew their
store, & say, that they must
vse their owne goods. Let
these first vnderstand, that
she is rich, who is rich in
God ; that she is wealthy
who is wealthy in Christ;
that those be goods indeed,
which be spirituall, diuine,
and heauenly, which lead
vs to god, which with sted-
fast possession remaine to
vs when we be with God.
But whatsoeuer things are
earthly, gotté in this world,
                    and

and heere to remaine within the world, they must be
contemned as well as the
world it self, whose pomps
and pleasures we doe then
renounce, when with a
better pace, we come to-
wards God. *S. Iohn* doth ex-
hort and stir vs vp, conte-
sting with his spirituall &
heauenly voice: *Do not,* saith
*he, loue the world, nor those things
which are in the world. If any
man loue the world, the Charity
of the Father is not in him, because all that is in the world, is
the concupiscence of the flesh, and
the concupiscence of the eyes, and*

Q 2   *the*

*the ambition of the world, which
is not of the Father, but of the
concupiscence of the world. And
the world shall passe, and the concupiscence therof. But he that doth
the will of God abideth for euer,
euen as God abideth for euer.*

Wherefore eternal &
diuine thinges are to be
sought after, and all things
are to be done according to
Gods will, that so we may
follow the footsteps of our
Lord, and his diuine ex-
examples, who did warne
vs and say: *I descended not from
heauen to do myne owne will, but
the will of him that sent me.*

Now

Now if the seruant be not greater then his Maister, & he that is made free oweth duety to his deliuerer, we that desire to be Christians, must imitate that which Christ did. It is written, it is read, it is heard, and for our example celebrated by the Churches mouth. He that sayth, he abideth in Christ, ought euen as he walked, himselfe also to walke. We must therefore walke with equal steps, we must endeauour to follow his paces. Then doth the following of the Truth, an-

Q3   swere

ſwere to the Faith of the
name, and reward is giuen
to him that belieueth, whē
that which is belieued is
alſo done .

Thou ſayſt, that ſhou
art wealthy and rich : but
S. Paul doth obiect againſt
thy riches, and preſcribe
with his wordes, that thy
trimming and decking is
to be moderated by an vp-
rightcous end. Let women
ſayth he, with ſhamfaſtnes
and modeſty adorne them-
ſelues, not in plaited hayre,
nor gold, nor pretious ſtons
nor gorgeous apparell , but

as

as it becōmeth women pro-
mising chastity by good
conuersation. *S. Peter* likewise doth consent with
these precepts and say: Let
there be in a woman, not
the outward decking of fai-
renes, or of gold, or of goodly garmentes, but the trimming of the hart. Now if
these men do admonish vs,
that euen those women ,
who are wont to excusethe
adorning of themselues for
their husbāds saks, are to be
restrained, and moderated
by religious obseruation,
according to Ecclesiasticall

disci-

difciplin: how much more
expedient is it that a Virgin
fhould obferue the fame?
Who deferueth no pardon
of this her trimming, neither can fhe caft her fault,
vpon another, but fhe her
felfe muftbeare all the bla-
me.

Thou doft fay, that thou
art wealthy and rich: but
not all that may, ought alfo
to be done. Neither muft
inordinate defires, and fuch
as fpring vp out of the ambition of the world, be ex-
tended beyond the honefty
& fhamfaftnes of a Virgin,
for

for so much as it is writen:
All thinges are lawfull, but
all thinges are not expedi-
dient. All things are lawfull, but all thinges do not
edify. But if thou adorne
thy selfe ouersumptuously,
and go abroad, so as al men
may note thee, and draw
the eyes of young men to
regard thee, and make them
sigh after thee, and nourish
their vnlawfull appetite to
desire thee, and kindle their
fire to longe after thee, in
such sort, that albeit thou
perish not thy selfe, yet thou
art the ruine of others, and
shew

shew thy selfe as a sword or poyson to those that looke on thee; thou canst not be excused, as if thou wert chast and honest in mind. Thy wanton attyre, and dishonest trimming doth reprehend thee; neither canst thou be numbred amongst the Damsels & Virgins of Christ, who dost liue so, as if thou wouldest be loued.

Thou dost say that thou art wealthy and rich; but it beseemeth not a virgin to vaunt of her riches, because holy scripture saith:

what

what good hath our pride
donne vnto vs , or what
profit hath the vaunting
of riches brought vs ? All
thofe things or paft away
like a fhadow . And againe
the Apoftle doth admonifh
vs and fay : And they that
buy, let them be as though
they poffeffed not; and they
that vfe this world , as
though they vfed it not : for
the figure of this world paf-
feth away. S. *Peter* alfo vnto
whome our Lorde mmé-
ded his fheepe to feed, and
to defend them , and vpon
whome he fet and founded
                         his

his Church, did denie that
he had either gold or filuer,
faying that he was rich in
the grace of Chrift , and
wealthy in his faith] and
power ; by which he could
do ftrange and miraculous
things, and by which he
abouded in fpirituall goods
to attain the grace of glory.
Thefe goods and riches fhe
can not poffeffe , who de-
fireth to be efteemed rich ,
rather to the world than to
Chrift. Thusfar S .*Cyprian.*

The fourth is her con-
uerfation, wherein the holy Fathers prefcribe to Virgins

gins, that they must auoyd
frequentation of marriages
publique banquettings, &
the company and conuersa-
tion of secular persons, especially of such are light in
their behauiour, and are
giuen vnto the world; and
that she should conuerse
with modest and deuout
women.

So saith *S. Cyprian* in the
place aboue cyted, *Quosdam
non pudet nubentibus interesse &c.*
Some (quoth he) are not a-
shamed to be preset at Marriages, and in that liberty of
lasciuious talke, to chatte
R   with

with the rest, and mingle
now and then , impure &
dishonest speaches; to heare
that which is not fitting to
be heard , nor lawfull to
speake againe;yea and to be
euen present at lasciuious
conferences , and drunken
banquets , by which the
fuell of Lust is kindled.
The Bride now accusto-
med to the patience of hea-
ring vnchastnes , and the
Bridegrome to be the more
audacious , what place is it
then to be at Marriages , for
such a one whose minde is
neuer to be marryed ? And
though

though she remaine both in
body & mind a virgin , yet
by her eares , and eyes, she
hathlost part of that which
she had before.

S. *Hierome* likewise in his
epist. to *Demetriades.* Decline
and auoyd (saith he) the
husbands of Matrons , such
as serue the world , for feare
least thy mind be troubled ,
and thou heare either what
the husband sayth to the
wife , or the wife to the
husband, for such Confe-
rences are poyson vnto o-
thers. Choose women that
are graue , and especially

R 2   Wid-

Widdowes and Virgins to
be thy companions, whose
conuersation is approued to
be good, their speaches well
gouerned; & their outward
modesty presages their san—
ctity within. Auoyd the
wantonnes and immodesty
of yong Maydes, who at-
tire their heads stangely,
weare lockes at their eares,
make their skynne smooth
by art, paint, weare straite
bodies, and sleeues, must
not haue a wrinkle in their
cloathes, weare creaking
shoes, and all thisforsooth,
that vnder the name of a
Mayde,

Mayde, they may seeme the more salable. For the comportment and inclination of the Mistresse, is oftentymes iudged and proportioned, by that of the wayting woman, and such as they keep company withal &c.

S. Hierome goeth on thus: And this likewise a Virgin must take specially heed of, that she neuer talke or couerse at any tyme alone, with any man, whether he be secular or religious, no not so much as with her ghostly Father, without the company of others: but

let all things be done openly, where they may be be-
held of others. Or if it be
neceſſary at any tyme to
talke with any man with-
in doors, let it not be done,
vnles ſome other be preſent
who may ſee al. For it is an
vnſeemly thing for a man,
thogh be her Confeſſarius,
yea religious(& though his
habit ſhould make him
ſeeme to be euen of the ſanctity of S. Iohn Baptiſt)to
be alone with a woman
in a chamber, the doore being ſhut, and without any
other preſent; whether it be
vnder

vnder pretense of Confessi-
on, or any spirituall instru-
ction whatsoeuer. Let her
remember that *Thamar* in
priuate, for want of presence of others, was rauished
by her owne brother. Let
her remember that for the
most part all that haue fallē
in this kind, haue done it
through the neglect of this
aduice.

If there were no confe-
rēce in priuat, there would
hardly any dishonesty be
euer committed. Therfore
this especially is to be obserued of a virgin, as a pre-

cept,

cept, That the keep herselfe
vndefiled, both before God
and men .

S. *Ambrose* also in his 2. bo.
vpon S. *Lukes* ghospell saith:
Trepidare virginum est &c. virgins ought to tremble and
feare, as often as any man
comes into their presence,
and be affrayde to speake
vnto any man &c. he spea-
keth of such a one when she
is alone (for in priuate they
are fire and tow to one another:) and the diuell neuer
more imployeth all his
strength and endeauour,
then at such a tyme, for
feare

feare leaſt ſo fit an occaſion
ſhould eſcape without be-
nefit vnto him. See more
concerning this matter in
S. *Hierome* in his 8.9.10.11.
and 22. Epiſtle.

Of any vow of Obedi-
ence to be made to ones
ghoſtly Father, I finde nothing written in holy Fa-
thers, neither do I iudg it
expedient (vnleſſe in ſome
few who are truly perfect,
& are become euen maiſters
as it were, in the way of
Perfection) by reaſon of
many diſcommodityes,
that may follow thereof.
Wher-

Wherfore it is deseruedly
forbiddē in the Rules of the
Society of Iesus , that any
such Vow should be admit-
ted by any Father of that
Order. To which also may
be added the solemne decre
of the Prouinciall Councel
of *Mechline* which by chāuce
I happened vpon lately ,
wherein the 5. tytle the 7.
Chap, are these words. *Nemo
aliquem ad perpetuò &c* . No
Ghostly father shall bynde
any one, neuer to confesse
his sinnes to any other then
to him &c. And this Synod
declareth all such Obligation

tion or promise, though
confirmed by vow, to be
vnreasonable, indiscreet,
voyd, and of no effect; &
therefore as far, as it shalbe
needfull, doth by this present Decree ordeyne it to
be so. I omit also many o-
ther things which may be
alleadged for this purpose.

These prescriptions of
holy Fathers, if a virgin
keep, liuing in the world,
she shall be happy, and her
Estate and condition shall
come neere to the perfectiõ
of a Religious life.

CHAP.

CHAP. VIII.

VVhether single life, confirmed by
Vow, may be properly
called an Estate.

SOME seeme to make
doubt, Whether single
life confirmed by vow, ought
properly to be called an E-
state; nor do I know vpon
what grounds. Neuertheles
it may be easily gathered
out of that which hath byn
layd before, that this manner of liuing, may be properly called an *Estate*, and
that

that such as professe the sam
may be rightly sayd to haue
chosen, and to be of an E-
state.

For an *Estate* is no-
thing els, but a manner of
life, in the which it is purposed so to cōtinue, that it
may not be lawfull to goe
out therof into another, as
S. Thom. 2. 2. quæst. 183. and
other Doctours, doe euery
where teach: but vowed
Chastity or Virginity is a
manner of life, wherein it
is firmely purposed to continue, so that it is not lawfull to forsake the same &

S   marry;

marry; therefore it is properly an Estate.

Henriques teacheth the
same in his 12 . *Quodlibet*,
where he sayth , That the
estate of Virginity or widdowhood is no lesse to be
accounted an Estate in the
Church of God , then the
Estate of Marriage . And
Caietan affirmeth, that this
doctrine of *Henriques* is true,
according to the Law , if
Virginity or Widdowhood
be kept, or professed by o-
bligation of vow .

And surely if there
be in the Church an Estate
of

of Marriage , why should there not be also an Estate of Virginity or widdow-hood? If there be an Estate of those which are wedded, why should there not be the like of those that liue continent, especially when S. *Cyprian* witnesseth ; *That this is the more beautyfull part or portion of Christ.* If marriage with a mortall man or wo-man, which can continue but a small tyme, setleth a man in an Estate , why should not also an eternall marriage with Christ him-self, which is neuer to haue

S 2   end,

end, effect the same ? Those
who at this prensent are in
the state of wedlocke, continue not longe therin, but
after a lirle time by death of
the one party, must go out
of it, into the estate of such
as liue single: but such as
are now in the Estate of
thos that liue continent,
shall neuer go out of it, but
alwayes remaine therein.
From whence it appeares
that this is rather, and more
perfectly to be tearned an
Estate, then that of Wed-
locke.

Neither doth it auaile,
that

that this vow of perpetuall
Virginity may be dispen-
sed with all, and that therfore this Estate seemeth not
to be firme & immoueable.
First, because such a dispen-
sation may be only graun-
ted by the Pope himselfe,
yea is very seldome graun-
ted, and that for matters of
great importance : other-
wise such release is not of
force before Almighty God;
but that which is only cō-
predended vnder the pow-
er of the Pope may be lawfully thought impossible to
vs, and therefore it dimini-

sheth

sheth not the immobility
or remouall of this estate:
for it is sufficient, that by vs
as much as is on our parts,
it is firme and immoueable,
in so much that it cannot
be altered by vs; otherwise
Religion it selfe shou'd not
be an Estate, since the Pope
may vpon iust occasions of
great importance, release a
Religious man from the o-
bligation of his Order, dif-
pense with his vowes, and
permit him to marry.

Secondly also, because
Marriage is an Estate, yet it
may be many wayes dissol-
ued,

ued, to wit before carnall knowledge of one another, by entring into Religion; and also after the knowledg of one another by death of the wife, or husband. Also by the Adultery of the husband, the wife hath right of a diuorce, whereby the Marriage it selfe is dissolued euen to euery ducty & coniugall act, as though it had beene no marriage at all, although the habituall obligation remaine.

Finally if it be contracted in the Estate of infidelity, it may be dissolued,

S 4   although

although it were consuma-
ted, by copulation, if so be
the one be conuerted to the
Catholike fayth, and the o-
ther perseuere in Infidelity.
Therefore Wedlocke is far
more easily, & more wayes
dissolued, then the vow of
Virginity: and yet that hindreth not, but that it is, and
may be truely called an E-
state; much lesse therefore
shal that power of releasing
it, which consisteth only in
the authority of the Prince
of spirituall matters, hinder the vow of Virg'nity of
being tearmed an Estate .

Third-

Thirdly a Cleargy-E-
state is made a true Estate
by meanes of the Vow of
Chastity, added to holy Orders, and hath sufficient fir-
menesse; and yet the Pope
may easily take it away, especially in a Deacon, and
giue him leaue to marry.
Therefore it followeth &c.

Lastly, Seruitude is a
true Estate, according to al
lawes, and yet at the Mai-
sters pleasure, the seruant
may be enfranchised, and
made free: Therefore that
extrinsecal power of taking
away any obligatiõ, which
con-

consisteth not in our owne powers, doth by no meanes impaire the assurednesse & certainty of an Estate . For it is inough, that it is firme and immutable on our part. And the reason is, because he is sufficiently sayd to be in an Estate, who maketh choice of a certaine kinde of life, and settleth himself firmely therein , so that he cannot take any other vpon him differet vnto this, but must continue therein , euen vnto death . But he who imbraceth single life, and byndeth himselfe by

vow

vow vnto it, chooseth to himselfe a certaine kind of life, & so establisheth him-selfe therein, as he cannot passe out of it, vnto the contrary. Therefore he is in an Estate.

You will aske perhaps, Whether this Estate may be called an Estate of Perfe-ction? I answere, that it is not a complete Estate of Perfectiō, but only in part, because it is a notable part of the Estate of perfectiōfor some Estates include more, & others lesse. An Estate of Perfection which is entire and

and complete, includeth also the vow of Pouerty and
Obedience, both which
a Virgin vowing Chastity
in the world, may also after
her manner, imitate and
supply before God.

FINIS.

THE
WIDDOWES
GLASSE.

ABRIDGED

Out of the Reuerend Father
Fuluius Androtius of
the Society of Iesus,
and others.

ANNO M. DC. XXI.

THE
PREFACE
TO ALL
deuout Widdowes.

ECAVSE
thou haſt loued
haſtity & re-
mained a Wi-
dow after ·hy husbãd, ·ther-
T 2 *fore*

fore the hand of our Lord hath strengthned thee, & thou shalt be blessed for euer. These wordes were spoken to the holy, vertuous, and renowned Widdow *Iudith,* who for her chast Widdowhood, deserued to be so strengthened of our Lord, that she ouercame, and killed the great and cruel *Holofernes,* deliuered the people of Israell from tribulation and death, and reduced

duced them to their for-
mer peace and tranquil-
lity.

And for this cause
did she also deserue to be
exalted to the Heauens,
by *Ioachim* the high Priest
who withall the people,
blessed her & sayd : *Thou
art the glory of Hierusalē,
thou the ioy of Israel, thou
the honour of our people,
because thou hast done man-
fully, and thy hart was
strēgthned from aboue &c.*

T 3   And

And befides all this, for her chaft Widdowhood did fhe merit an euerlafting bleffing from our Lord, to wit, aboundance of all graces in this world, and perfect felicity in heauen.

In like manner, all vertuous Widdows following thefe her traces and footfteps, fhall deferue to be côforted by our Lord with fpirituall graces, vertues, and gifts of the holy

holy Ghoſt, in ſuch ſort,
that they ſhalbe euer bleſſed and happy, if deuout-
ly they perſeuere in their
chaſt Widowhood, & ſhal
alſo deſerue to ouercome
& trample the diuell vn-
der foot, ſignifyed by the
aforeſayd proud and cru-
ell Captaine *Holofernes* .
And to the end, that they
may thus conſtantly and
deuoutly perſeuere in the
holy Eſtate of Continē-
cy in their widdowhood,

T 4   we

we will, with the help of
the holy Ghoſt, ſay ſome-
thing to this purpoſe, as
as wel out the holy Scrip.
tures, as ancient Fathers
and Hiſtoryes.

THE

THE WIDDOWES GLASSE.

CHAP. I.

VVho are to be accounted truely VViddowes.

THERE are sayd to be three kindes of Chastity, to wit, that of Marriage, that of Widdowes, & that of Virgins: al three signi-

signifyed by the good groūd
mentioned in the Holy
Ghospell, wheron the seed
fell : The first wherof yiel-
ded fruit thirthy sould, the
second sixty sould, and the
last an hundred. But they
who cannot yeild the hun-
dred-fould fruit, let them at
least offer vp sixty, to shew
themselues more liberall towards our Sauiour .

And for as much as
all perfection of man consisteth in abandoning and
forsaking carnal and worldly things, & drawing neer
and ioyning himselfe vnto
God

God his Creatour, louing
him, fearing him, seeking
him, thinking on him, con-
templating and honouring
him in euery thing and a-
ction; this can hardly be affected in the state of Marriage, especially by womē,
who hunting after, & day-
ly following the delightes
and pleasures of the world,
are hindred thereby, for the
most part, from treading the
true path which leadeth di-
rectly thereunto. But Widdowes who are free from
such cares and troubles, and
haue a true defire, may with
great

great cafe and facility performe the fame to their
great comfort.

Now, there be diuers
forts of Widdowes. Some,
as foone as their hufbands
be dead, purpofe fo marry
againe, for fome temporall
comfort and confolation,
not hauing any diuine In-
fpiration to ferue God Almighty in that Eftate, and
are in danger to offend him.
Of this fort of widdowes
S . Paul fpeaketh when he
faith. *I will, that the* ᵛong *wid-*
dowes do marry againe, & become
mothers of families, not to giue oc-
cafion

casion to the Diuell to tempt them.
And this is not ill but approued of all . But when
a widdow will marry a-
gaine for any disordinate
appetit , or because she is
very rich, or faire, or soght
after by some one that is
placed in a high degree of
Honour or State, or for any
other vicious occasion, or ill
end, without doubt this her
desire is naught , nor is she
to be reckoned, or worthily
called a widdow , as long
as she remaynes with this
desyre , although she do not
actually marry againe .

V   There

There is another ſort of
widdowes , who though
they do not purpoſe to marry againe at all, eyther for
that they haue no dowry,
or for feare leaſt they happen vpon an ill husband,or
for ſome other ſecret or ma-
nifeſt reſpect , yet is their
manner of life and conuerſation, not like indeed vnto
widdowes : for that they
will allwayes be gadding
abroad , tatling, & goſſip-
ping, euen with thoſe who
be not reputed of the beſt
edification . And theſe ,
forſooth, will be finely ap-
parelled

parelled : and though they
haue veyles , yet will they
ſcarſely couer their heades
with them; their eyes muſt
be rolling vp and downe,
they muſt go to banquets
weddings and playes , they
muſt tell tales , heare & tell
newes , & carry themſelues
euen as meere ſecular , ordi-
nary , and the worſt ſort of
people. Theſe are to be auoyded and ſhunned by all true
widdowes : and theſe be
thoſe of whome S. Paul ſpeaketh in another place , ſaying : *Take heed of ſuch yonge*
widdowes, for after that they haue
V 2 *liued*

liued riotously, and licentiously in
Christ, they will marry, carrying
with them their damnation, for
that they haue broken and made
voyd their first faith. &c . And
for these it were better that
they did marry againe, then
liue as they do.

Another sort there is ,
who neuer intend, nor do
indeed marry againe , but
liue chastely & vertuously,
both in act and desyre . But
yet they do it not for the
loue of God , but rather for
some humaine respect , as
for the loue of their childré,
their goods, or the like. And
                            although

although according to the
esteeme of the world, they
liue honestly, and are reputed for Venerable Mo-
thers and Matrones ; yet
are they wholy dedicated to
the seruice of the world, &
haue little feeling or gust
of spirituall things; and do
but seldome frequent the
Sacraments or sermons, fast
only but when the church
commandeth them, or doe
imploy themselues in any
other spirituall Exercises.
These I do intreat, by the
bowels of Christ Iesus, that
they will no longer imploy

the gifts and graces which
they haue receaued frō our
Lord, to the honour and
seruice of the world, to the
end they may haue their
reward in heauen, and not
on earth.

There is another sort of
widdowes also, who make
a firme purpose and deli-
beration, to conserue and
keep their chastity & serue
God with all their hart: &
of these there are two kinds.
One who cannot separate
themselues from their children, or other parents, ci-
ther for the charge they
haue

haue of thé, or becaufe they
cannot fo wel liue alone, or
for fome neceffity, or charity in gouerning their family: and thefe although they
be not wholy free from the
world, nor are dedicated to
the feruice of God ; not-
withftanding al the paynes
and lábours they take, they
doe it principally for the
loue of God, of whom they
fhalbe rewarded with life
euerlafting . Thefe Wid-
dowes are not any to be re-
moued , or drawne away
from this kind of life , but
are, according to S. *Paul*,
V 4 greatly

greatly to be honoured and
esteemed.

The other kind, are
those Widdowes, who de-
sirous to serue God, & may
commodiously separat thē-
selues from their parents,
friends, or family, and be
more free to attend to prayer and other deuout exercises; yet they will not, thorough a kind of pusillani-
mity, or little courage, or
els for compassion to their
friendes, or for some other
reason. Neither are these
to be condemned, but esteemed in a second, or third
degree

degree from the former.

The last sort of widdow-
es, are the true, & worthily
so called, Widdowes, who
dispatching themselues of
al worldly impedimēts, do
attend only to the seruice
of God, cōtemplating him,
and meditating on him day
and night. And these are
placed in a more quiet and
peaceable Estate, then any
of the others aboue named,
and are entred into the
right, and direct way of
perfection.

In this Estate liued that
Holy Widdowe *Anne* the
Prophetesse,

Prophetesse, recorded by
S. *Luke*; who is sayd to
haue serued God in fasting
& prayer, remaining night
and day in the Temple. And
if such Widdowes, who
haue a desire to liue vertu-
ously cánot match or come
neere to S. *Anne*; yet let thé
come as neere vnto her as
they can.

So as I conclude, that the
true Widdow, is she, who
not only conserues her
Chastity in the world, but
also whatsoeuer she doth,
she doth it purely for the
honour and seruice of Al-
mighty

mighty God. And for that
euery widdow doth not
know how to exerciſe her
ſelfe in the truly ſeruing of
God, vnleſſe ſhe know the
ſcope and end therof, I purpoſe heere to ſet downe
briefly in what manner ſhe
is to do the ſame.

CHAP. II.

Of the Intention, and Exerciſe
of a true VViddow.

VVHEN a Widdow
hath well conſi-
dered of her Eſtate & firme
purpoſe to ſerue God, it is
neceſſary, that firſt ſhe vn-
derſtand

derstand what is the end &
scope of this kind of life,
that conformably therto,
she may addresse all her
workes and actions.

The first and principal
end then is, that not onely
Widdowes but euery Chri-
stian also ought to liue wel
and in the feare of God,
whome she must loue more
then her owne soule: and
therefore she must labour,
that by al her endeauours &
actions the name of God
may be euer blessed & praised, Christian fayth and religion aduanced, and ho-
nou-

noured . This belongeth
more to Widdowes then to
many others, who confe-
quently muft be mortifyed,
and of a chaft and pure life .
For that they hauing loft
their carnall Spoufes, they
ought to feeke for no other
but their Spoufe Chrift Iefus. So as a truely deuout
Widdow ought fo to infla-
me her hart with the zeale
of Gods honour, that fhe
fhould choofe rather to dye,
then that by her means, her
Spoufe fhould be any way
difhonoured .

Secondly fhe ought with
X   as

as great zeale seek and procure her owne saluation,
considering that she is not
alwayes to remayne in this
world, because it is ordayned for al men once to dye,
and then of necessity, to go
either to heaue, or to intol-
lerable torments in Hell,
or Purgatory. And there-
fore hauing as it were, lost
and forgone all the Conso-
lations of this transitory
world, she must force her
self, to get & conserue those
that be celestiall, and euerlasting.

CHAP.

CHAP. III.
Documents for VViddowes out of
S. Paul.

SAINT *Paul* wryting to *Timothy* sayth : *Honour VViddowes.* He meaneth such Widdowes who liue vertu-ously according to the rule of Widdow-hood, that is to say, to gouerne wel their families, not onely their chil-dren, or their kinsfolkes, but also their subiects, in-structing them in good life, manners and vertue, and when it is needfull to re-prehend and correct them.

Secondly

Secondly he ſayth, That Widdowes ought to hope in God, to truſt in his mercy ; in him alone to ſeeke for Comfort and conſolation , hauing dayly their mind cleuated in God in al humility , praying often , and imploring his diuine ayde to preſerue them from all euill, to forgiue them , (and all ſinners) their ſins, to repleniſh them with his gifts and graces, and laſtly to guide them to eternall felicity.

Thirdly he ſayth, That a VViddow entertayning

world-

worldly & carnall consola-
tions, & passing her dayes
in mirth, ioylity, & vanity
is accompted for dead. For
although she liue according
to the body, yet is she dead
according to the spirit; nor
can she once do any good or
meritorious work, worthy
of heauen.

Fourthly, he comman-
deth widdowes, That they
should be irreprehensible in
all their words and deeds;
that is to say, that in all
their actiōs they giue good
example, & that they keep
themselues, not only from

cōmitting of mortai crims, but euen from the least veniall sinnes that may be. Whence it followes, that if they liue vertuously, hūbly, in feare and vigilancy, it may be said of them, as it was said of *Iudith*, that most noble and deuout widdow, *That neuer was there foūd any man who spake euill of her*.

Fiftbly he sayth, That the Widow ought to think vpon those things that belong vnto God, to the end she may be holy & sanctifyed in body and spirit &c.

CHAP.

C H A P. IIII.

The prayse of VViddowhood, out of S. Hierome.

SAINT *Hierome*, amongst the rest of Ancient Fathers, is not the last, nor least that hath praysed widdowhood ; nay I may say, he hath exalted the same aboue many, if not aboue all the rest. And to begin first with an Epistle of his to *Furia*, a Noble yong Lady and widdow of Rome ; thus he wryteth vnto her in cōmendation of the crown of Widdowhood.

X 4   You

You defire in vour letter,
and humbly intreate me ,
that I will anfwere you ,
or rather write vnto you
in what manner you may
liue,& conferue the crowne
of widdowhood, without
any blemifh of the honour
of your good Name. My
mind reioiceth,my bowells
do daunce , my affection
doth leape, becaufe you defire to be fuch after your
hufbandsdeath,as your mo-
ther *Titiana* of holy memory
was a long time her hufbād
liuing . Her praiers and deuotions are heard. She hath
obtai-

obtained in her onlydaugh-
ter, that which she possessed
whilest she liued.

You haue moreouer a ve-
ry great Priuiledge of your
Ancestours, that euen from
Camillus , either none at all,
or very few women of your
stocke was married the second time : so that you are
not so much to be praised,
if you remain a widdow;as
to be detested , if being a
Christian , you performe
not that , which heathen
women for so many ages
haue obserued. I say nothing
of *Paula* & *Eustochiū* , flowers
of

of your family, leaft I may
feeme to take occafion by
the exhorting of you, to
praife them. I let paffe *Blefilla*
which following her hus-
bád your brother, in a fhort
fpace of life, fulfilled many
yeares of vertue.

And I would to God
that men would imitate the
praifes of women, & wrin-
ckled ould age would per-
forme that which volun-
tary youth doth offer. Wit-
tingly & willingly I thruft
my hand into the fire. Many
countenances wil frowne,
many armes will be fpread
abroad,

abroad, and angry *Chremes*
will rage with his foa-
ming mouth. Many great
perfonages will be incenfed
againft my Epiftles : the
whole company of Nobles
will thunder out, and fay
I am a witch, that I am a
feducer, worthy to be ba-
nifhed from all ciuill common wealthes. Let them
adde, if they will, a Sama-
ritane alfo, that I may acknowledge my Lords title.

Surely, I do not deuide
the daughter from her fa-
ther Neither do I fay that
of the gofpell, Suffer the
dead.

to bury the dead. For whosoeuer beleeueth in Christ
liueth, and whosoeuer be-
leueth in him, ought surely
to walke, euen as he wal-
ked. Honour your father,
but so, as he seuere you not
from your true father. So
long acknowledg the linck
of your bloud, how long he
acknowledgeth his Crea-
tour. For otherwise Dauid
will presently sing vnto
you: Heare O daughter, &
see, and incline thine eare,
and forget thy people, and
the house of thy father : and
the King will desire thy
beauty

beauty, becaufe he is thy
Lord, thy God, and thy
King.

O great reward of for-
getting ones Father! The
King wil defire thy beauty:
becaufe thou haft heard, becaufe thou haft feene, becaufe thou haft inclined thy
eare, & forgot thy people
and the houfe of thy father;
therfore will the King defire thy beauty, and will fay
vnto thee: Thou are al faire,
O my Deare, and there is
no fpotte in thee. What
thing more faire then the
foule, which is called the

Y   daughter

daughter of God, and seeketh no forraine ornaments: she beleeueth in Christ, and with this ambition she goeth to her spouse, hauing the same to her Lord, and to her spouse.

What miseries mariage haue, you haue learned in marriage it selfe: and you haue bene filled with that which you longed for, euen vnto loathsomenes. Your iawes haue tryed most bitter choler, you haue cast out those sower & vnwholsom meates, you haue eased your boyling stomake. Why wil you

you yet throwe in againe
that which once was hurt-
full vnto you ? The dogge
returneth to his vomit, and
the sow againe to her wal-
lowing in the mire . The
very brute beastes, & restles
birdes, do not fall the secōd
time into the same snares &
nettes.

Do you feare least the
family of the *Furij* be extinguished, and least your father haue not a babe by
you, which may creepe in
his bosome, and bestraue his
necke ? What, I pray you,
haue all which are maried,

children ? And those children which they haue, do they alwaies answere to their kinred ? Yea surely *Ciceroes* sonne did resemble his fathers eloquence : and *Cornelia* your Auncestresse, an example of honesty and fecundity, had much ioy of the *Gracchi* her sonnes. It is ridiculous to hope of a certainty for that, which both many haue not had, & haue lost when once they had it.

To whom wil you leaue so great riches ? To Christ who cannot dye. Who shall be your heire ? he which is
also

also my Lord. Your father
will mourne, but Chrift
will reioyce; your family
will be forowfull, but the
Angels will be ioyfull. Let
your father do what he wil
with his fubftance: you are
not his, by whom you were
borne, but his by whom
you were borne againe, and
who redeemed you with an
exceeding great price, euen
with his bloud.

So far, ould good S.
Hierom. Where you fee what
efteeme he maketh of Wid-
dowhood, yea in a young,
noble, and beautifull Lady.

Y 3   And

And no lesse doth he in another Epistle of his to *Marcella*, commending the courage and resolution of *Blesilla* a young & Noble widdow also. Thus then he
writeth to *Marcella* of *Blesilla* her sicknes.

Abraham is tempted in
his soone, & is found more
faithfull. Ioseph is sould
into Ægipt, that so he may
feed his father & brethren.
Ezechias is terrified with
his death at hand, and dissolued into teares, hath his
life prolonged for fifteene
yeares. Peter the Apostle is
afflicted

afflicted, with our Lords
passion, and weeping bit-
terly, he heareth; Feed my
sheepe . Paul a rauening
woolf, and another young
Beniamin is stroken blind
in a traunce, that he may
receiue his sight: and being
compassed with a suddaine
horrour of darknes, calleth
him Lord, whom before he
persecuted as man .

Euen so now, O *Marcella*,
we haue seene our louing
Blæsilla thirty daies continually to haue bene tormented
with the burning of an
ague, that she might learne

Y 4   to

to reiect the delights of that body which shortly after is to be consumed with wormes. To her also came our Lord Iesus, and touched her hand, and behould the arising, now serueth him. She sauoured somewhat of negligence: and being tied with the bandes of riches, she lay in the sepulcher of the world. But Iesus groned, and being troubled in spirit, cried out: *Blesilla*, come forth. Who arose when she was called, and being come forth, now sitteth at the table with our Lord.

Let

Let the Iewes threaten
and swell , let them seeke
to murder her who hath
bene raised vp againe ; and
let the oly apostles reioyce.
She knoweth, that she
oweth her life vnto him,
who did restore it . She
knoweth that she ebraceth
his feete , whose iudgment
lately she feared. Her body
lay almost dead : and death
approaching did shake her
gasping members . Where
were then the helpes of her
kinred ? where were then
the wordes full of vanity ?
She oweth nothing vnto
thee

thee O vngratefull kinred,
which dying to the world
is reuiued vnto Chrift.
Who is a Chriftian, let him
reioyce: he that is angry,
fheweth that he is no Chriftian.

A widdow loofed from
the bond of marriage, nee-
deth nothing but perfeue-
rance: But doth the courfe
garment offend any perfon?
let Iohn offend him, then
whom, amongft the fonnes
of women there was none
greater: who being called
an Angell, baptized our
Lord himfelfe, for he alfo

was

was claod with a Camells
skynne, and girded with a
girdle of hayre . Do groſſe
meates diſpleaſe them? nothing is more groſſe then
locuſts . Let thoſe women
rather offend Chriſtian eies
who with verniſh and co-
lours paint their eies, and
cheekes : whoſe plaiſtered
coūtenance deformed with
ouermuch ſhining, doth re-
ſemble Idols . Who if they
happen for want of heed to
let fall a teare, it trickleth
downe in a furrow: whom
not ſo much as the very
number of their yeares can
perſwade

perswade that they are old : who with other folkes hair set forth their head : and paint out in aged wrinckles their youth forespent: who finally in presence of many nephews are trimmed like trembling girles.

Let the Christian woman blush, if shee force the comelinesse of nature, if she make prouision for the flesh vnto concupiscence, in which according to the Apostle, whosoeuer are delighted, cannot please God. Our widow before was very carefully dressed: and all the

the day at the glasse she stu-
died what might be amisse.
Now she confidently saith:
but we beholding the glory
of our lord with face reuea-
led, are transformed into
the same image, from glory
vnto glory, as of our Lords
spirit. Then the maides did
platte her hayre , and the
harmeles head was wrin-
ged with frizcled tops : but
now the vntrimmed head
knoweth this to suffice, that
it is couered .

Then did the very soft-
nes of feathers seeme hard ,
and she could scarce lay in

Z   the

the raysed bedds : now she
riseth betimes for to pray,
and with her shrill voice
preuenting the others, in
singing *Alleluia*, she is the first
which beginneth to prayse
her Lord. She kneeleth v-
pon the bare ground, and
with often teares that face
is purged, which before
was defiled with painting.
After prayer, there are sung
psalmes : & the feeble neck,
and wearyed knees, & slee-
py eyes, for the earnest feruour of the mind, can scant
obtain any rest. The mourning gowne is least souled,
when

when she lyeth on the
ground. The course pan-
tofile affoardeth the price
of gilt shoes vnto the poore:
the girdle is not beset with
gold & pretious stones, but
of wollen, and most pure,
because of the simplicity,
& such as may rather strai-
ten the garments, then a-
dorne them.

If the Scorpion enuy-
eth so good a purpose, and
with flattering speach perswade againe to eate of the
forbidden tree; insteed of
a shoe, let him be crushed
with a curse; & whilest he

Z2   dyeth

dyeth in his poyſon let him
haue this anſwere: Go after
me Satan: which is as much
to ſay, as Aduerſary; for he
is the Aduerſary of Chriſt,
and an Antichriſt, whoſoe-
uer is diſpleaſed with the
precepts of Chriſt.

I pray you, what haue
we done likevnto the Apo-
ſtles, that they are ſo offended? They forſake their a-
ged Father with their ſhip
and nets: the Publican ri-
ſeth from the cuſtom-houſe
& followeth our Sauiour:
The diſciple which deſired
to returne home, and bidd
          his

friends farewell, is forbidden by our Maiſters voice.
The buriall of a Father is
not allowed, & it is a kind
of piety, for our Lord to be
voyd of pitty. We, becauſe
we goe not in ſilkes, are e-
ſteemed Monks, becauſe we
are not drunke, neither o-
pen our mouthes vnto diſ-
ſolute laughter, we are cal-
called graue and melancho-
ly. If our coate be not gorgeous, we ſtraight heare
that common Prouerbe: He
is an hypocrite, and deccea-
uing Grecian.

  Let them vſe euen yet
  Z 3   more

more rude fcoffes;and carry about with them men ftuffed with fat paunches. Our *Blefilla* will laugh, and not difdaine to hear the reproaches of croking frogges, whereas her Lord & Maifter was called *Beelzebub*.

    Hitherto S. *hierome.* And there might be heer fet downe many of his Epiftls of the fame fubiect in praife and commendation of the Crowne and Merit of Widdowhood, if this litle treatife were capable therof, or that it were our intention to make heereof a great volume.

lume. And therfore we wil
content our felues at this
tyme with fome briefe Ad-
uertifementes of his, concerning the fame fubiect.

CHAP. V.

Aduertifementes to VViddowes,
out of the fame S. Hicrome

MANY are the Inftru-
ctions & documents,
which the ancient Fathers,
haue fet down for vertuous
& deuout Widdowes. And
firft of all we will produce
what we find written by S.
Hierome aforefayd in diuers
places of his works, in the
Z 4   brie-

briefest manner we can, not
to ouerweary the Widdow-
Reader.

As those Widdowes
(sayth S. *Hierome*) who whē
they were marryed, did only study to please their husbands: so let those, who are
now freed from carnal marriage, seeke and study only
to please God, whome they
haue chosen for their spouse
in place of their former husbands.

As Widdowes whilest
they were ioyned to the
world, did vse the vanity of
the world: so let them now
                    being

being ioyned to god, banish
from their hartes all vanityes.

As Widdowes, whi-
lest they were marryed in
the world, studyed how to
nourish and pamper their
bodyes, for the bearing of
children, & supporting the
burden of Marriage: so now
let them keep sobriety, and
bring their body into seruitude, and subiect the same
to the spirit, thereby to be
able to serue their second
spoule Christ Iesus, in their
sacred and spirituall Marriage.

Lee

Let a Widdow be so
much the more a louer of
Chastity; by how much all
her actions , wordes , and
workes, may sauour of pu-
rity .

Let her neuer be alone,
as neere as possible, with
any man, that she need not
be ashamed , whensoeuer
she is seen to conuerse with
another.

Let her alwayes a-
uoyd the compny of vaine,
idle, and sensuall persons;
especially of Widdows that
should be so giuen : nor so
much as permit any such to
come

come neere vnto her.

Let her take great heed neuer to detract, or murmure, or speake euill of any man. Let her also auoyd those who vse to murmure, and permit them not vpon any occasion to speake euill of any person in her presence, to the end that those who visit her, may be edifyed by her vertuous comportment.

She must also haue a great care of her honesty and reputation, of which she ought to be alwayes so iealous, and fearefull, that

her

her fpeach , her face , and
all the actions of her body,
yea her very garments may
demonftrate the fame; to
the end that no occafion be
giué to others , not fo much
as to thinke the contrary of
her.

By how much more
younge fhe is; by fo much
the more ought fhe to be
graue, and venerable in all
her actions.

Let her not take too
much pleafure, or delight in
finging, efpecially of fongs;
but let her recreate her felfe
honeftly with thofe of her
owne

owne house and family.

Let her alwayes haue at
hand, some book of deuotion; & let her haue often re-
course vnto prayer, which
is the readiest way to driue
away all vayne and euill
thoughts, which the Ene-
my may put into her mind.

And for that, the flesh
hath continually combat
with the spirit, let her vse
abstinence, and other mortifications, to subdue the
same, according to the coū-
sell of her prudent Ghostly
Father.

As Anger and Choller is
A a   natu-

naturall oftentymes to a man : so neuer to be ouer-come therwith is most pro-per to a Christian . Let the widdow therfore take great heed therof .

Let her alwayes haue be-fore her eyes the examples of *Indith,* and *Anne* the Pro-phetesse , widdowes , who continually night and day imployed their tyme in prayer , fasting , and vertu-ous exercises . For which God gaue to one of them so much grace and valour , as to ouercome and cut off the Diuels head, figured in that

of

of *Holofernes* ; and to the o-
ther, to be the firſt widdow
who ſhould imbrace, and
receaue the Sauiour of the
world in her armes, and
thereby made partaker of
diuers diuine ſecrets.

Let her conſider that her
ſoule, is the daughter of
God, & therfore ſhe ought
not to vſe any ſtrang or fan-
taſtical ornaments to adorn
her body ; but let all her
ſtudy and care be to adorne
her ſoule, as it becommeth
the daughter of God,

She muſt not content
her ſelfe to haue begon any

thing well, but she must study how to end it well: although *S. Paul* began to do euill, and ended with good; and *Iudas* contrariwise began to do well, but ended in euill.

To what purpose should there be colours & vernice vsed, to paint the face of a Christian? Such an ornament of the body becommeth not one, that serueth Christ, but rather one who serueth Antichrist. And if any looke towardes heauen with such a face, Christ wil not know them, since they

haue

haue changed that shape
which he gaue them.

Why do we promise
one thing, and do another?
And why doth the tongue
prayse Chastity, & the body exercise Impurity?

It is a very great ver-
tue, & worthy to be sought
after with great diligence,
care, and watchfullnes, to
wit, to be born in the flesh,
& not to liue according to
the flesh.

If S. Paul feared, say-
ing: *I doe not the good that I
would, and therefore I do bring
my body into servitude*. Which

A a 3   of

of vs is there, who can be assured in this case?

If *Dauid* and *Salomon*, the familiar friendes of God, haue beene ouercome, by the temptations of their flesh: who is he, that will not feare to fall, walking vpon so slippery an yce?

Let a widdow continually thinke of doing seriously the will of God, that she may be worthy often to heare that saying of our Sauiour in the Ghospell: *Not those who say lord, lord, shall enter into the kingdome of heauen, but those who shall doe the will of my Father*

Father which is in heauen. And that also which he sayd in another place: *VVhy do yee call me Lord and Maister, and do not the thinges I command you to do?* And againe: *He that doth the will of my Father, is my brother, my sister, and my Mother.*

Moreouer God saith by his Prophet: *The Sonne honours the Father, and the seruant the Maister: But I am your Father, and where is my honour? I am your Maister, and where is my seruice?* Wherby it is manifest that whosoeuer doth not the will of God, nor loues him as a Father, nor

A a 4   serue

serues and feares him as a
Lord and Maister, is (as holy *Dauid* fayth) for that he is
a sinner, & hath done euil.

Labour, that thou
mayst be rich: but so, as the
poore may gaine thereby.
And it wilbe most pleasing
to God, if thou giue what
thou canst possibly spare to
the poore.

VVhensoeuer a widd-
ow takes her repast, let her
thinke on the poore, if she
be of ability; at least let her
giue what she can, accor-
ding to her riches, or pouerty. And let her also think

at

at this tyme, that by and by
after ſhe muſt fall to her
prayers, or read ſome good
ſpirituall leſſon, or exerciſe
her ſelfe about ſome other
deuout and pious worke.

VVhileſt a Widdow
hath meanes, let her make
vnto her ſelfe friendes by
Almes; that when the ſame
is wanting, and all ſpent,
they may receaue her into
the euerlaſting tabernacles.

Giue vnto all thoſe that
ſhall demand of you, if you
be able, and ſpecially to
thoſe who be good. Cloath
the naked, feed the hun-
gry

gry, and visite the sicke.

Euery tyme that you stretch forth your hand, to giue to the poore, remember that it is Iesus Christ to whome you giue: and behold, how your sweet lord, and Sauiour beggeth, to lay vp riches for you, against you haue need.

Think often that within a short tyme, you are to dye, and leaue this world; and so, you shall haue little list to thinke of a second worldly marriage.

Carry your selfe so, in the gouernement of your house

houte and family, that all
may acknowledge you for
their Miftreffe ; and alfo re-
uerence you for your holy
and vertuous life.

Fly all forts of perfons,
that haue any fufpitiõ of an
euil name ; it is not inough
to fay, *My Confcience is cleer I
care not what others fay of me* :
but take you away all occafion from others of thin-
king ill, wherby God may
be in any fort offended.

Seeke firft of all the
kingdome of heauẽ purely ,
and all other thinges ne cef-
fary fhall be giuen vnto you
aboun-

aboundantly.

A VViddow ought to flye all inordinate delights of the sense of Tasting: and for this cause, God would not haue hony to be burnt in his honor in the church, but oyle, which comes from the bitter Oliue-tree, and is of an vnpleasant tast.

S. *Paul* did chastise and afflict his body diuersly, that he might not become reprobate. And who will warrant a young widdow for her Chastity, if she continually fill her belly with variety of delicate viands?

It

It is not possible, that any one now adayes should be exempted frō the obliquy of mens tongnes, since it is become, as it were, a kind of pastime among the bad, to speake euill of the good: but a false bruite is soone past; and this present life of ours, doth giue vs witnesse of our life past. If any speake ill of thee, amend thy fault, and the rumour will quickly cease.

Nobility, Beauty, yong Age and Riches, make wid-dowes amiable vnto euery one; And how many more

enemyes they haue to fight
against, for the conseruation of their Chastity ; so
much more great shall be
their reward and recom-
pence, if they másully resist
and ouercome.

Fly the company of
those widdowes, who are
widdowes not in will, but
of a kind of necessity; as also
those who liue in such sort,
that they may seeme not to
haue lost their husbands.

God did not send a wid-
dow riches to be idle, or to
spend the same vnthriftile,
but rather to the end she
might

might labour the more, eſ-
pecially with her owne
hands, and to haue dayly
ſomthing to giue therof to
the poore.

Haue continually before
your eyes, and in your memory, this ſentence: *That
which you would haue to be done
vnto your ſelues, do you the ſame
vnto another.*

Do not eaſily beleeue
euill of another, for this
is the property of a light &
giddy mind, which for this
reaſon is ſeldome in quiet.

Do not regard that which
another prayſeth in thee;

B b 2   but

but weigh and ponder the
same well with thy selfe, &
in thy owne conscience.

Speake little , and not
without necessity, & thou
shalt auoyde a number of
sinnes and imperfections.

Esteeme nothing more
amiable, or precious, then
Humility which is the keeper & guardian of all other
vertues. And know, that
ther is nothing which ma-
kes thee more regarded of
God and men, then Humi-
lity, our sweet Sauiour saying : *In whome shall I repose or
rest, but in the humble ?*

This

This Humility muſt not be exteriourly faygned, nor in wordes only; but truly perfect, and in the hart: for the Pride, which is turned into Humility, is extreme deformed: and the vices with are couered ouer with the veyle of Vertue, are inſupportable, & odious in the ſight of God.

Do not preferre thy ſelf, before another, eyther for that thou art Noble, Rich, or Fayre, or for any other exteriour ornament of thy body: but rather eſteeme thy ſelfe the more baſe and
Bb 3   abiect

abiect, therby to be truly greater in the sight of God. For we are all borne of the same parents *Adam* & *Euen*, and all redeemed with the selfe same bloud of Iesus Christ.

Do not regard the conditions of persons, but their affections: for their māners and carriage make them as well base, as noble. It is true liberty, and noblenes indeed, according to God, not to be a slaue to sinne. Who hath byn more famous or illustrious then *S. Peter*, who was cuē but a poore Fisherman?

man? Who among women
hath been more noble then
the B. Virgin, who was neuerthelesse espoused but to
a poore Carpenter? To this
Fisherman, God notwith-
standing gaue the keyes of
Heauen: and this humble
Virgin was made worthy
to be the Mother of God
himselfe, and her spouse
S. *Ioseph* his Foster-Father.

Haue some conuenient &
retyred place in thy house
whither thou maist repayre
often to talke & trait with
God alone, as well about
that which belongeth to

B b 4   thy

thy felfe, as to thy family.

Content thy felfe to haue
loft the firft degree of Virginity; & that by the third,
thou art come to the fecōd:
to wit, that by the endea-
nour of marriage, thou art
come to the continency of
Widdow-hood.

Many women whilft
their hufbands are aliue,
make vowes of Chaftity &
are continent. And fhall not
others who are freed from
their hufbands, and are become widdowes, much
fooner performe the fame?

God gaue thee a husbād,
and

and God hath taken him
from thee againe, & therby
made thee free from the ſeruitude of men . Do thou
therfore reder him due thã-
kes by thy chaſt and vertuous liuing in widdowhood

Let the yong widdow,
who cannot (or rather will
not) liue chaſt, rather take a
husband, then the diuell.

Yow know by experience
how many troubles cares &
anguiſhes of mynd marrya-
ge drawes with it : Now
that you haue vomitedvp al
the bitterneſſe therof, wherfore will you be againe
caught

caught with the same? The byrd, that hath once had her foot in the limer wigs, wil take heed for comming there againe, I trow.

Make a Vertue of Necessity: and leaue not a thing certaine, for an vncertayne if you be wise.

Take heed of the coūsells of your Nurse, and others of your house and family, for that they do alwayes set before your eyes somthing that may please yow, and that may turne to their owne profit & cōmodity.

If

If in doing well your Father, or carnal friends be heauy and grieued, your Spouse Christ Iesus will reioyce: And if your family weepe, the Angells will singe.

You do not so much belong to those of whom you were borne, as to him of whome yow were regenerat, & borne a new; redeemed by his pretious bloud and death.

Let the yong Widdow, if her stomacke be weake, vse a little wyne ; but let her take heed of meates that be

hoate

hoat of nature.

A Heathen women once
said, *He that had my first loue,
was my husband: and he that hath
take it away, let him keep it with
him still in his graue.* If an In-
fidell did so much dispraise
and dislike a second mar-
riage: what shall be expe-
cted that a Christian widdow should do?

All these sayings are of
good old S. *Hierome*: in ga-
thering wherof I haue byn
the longer, for that I hope
they wil be pleasing & cō-
fortable to widdows. Now
let vs see a little what S. *Augustine*

guſtine will ſay vnto vs, concerning the ſame ſubiect.

C H A P. VI.

*Documents for VViddowes, out of
S·. Auguſtine.*

T H E widdow that
hath Children, ought
to bring them vp, and in-
ſtruct them in the feare of
God. And this muſt be her
principall care . Neither
ought ſhe ſo much to glory
that ſhe hath children, as
that ſhe hath indeed good
and vertuous children.

If ſhe reſolue to keep her
C c   wid-

dowhood , let her giue
thankes to good, who hath
by his holy infpiration ,
put this relolution into her
hart, & let her in all things
praife his holy Name .

Let her not defpife thofe
who haue not the intentiõ
to remayne widdowes:but
let her know , that it is a
fpeciall gift of God ; and
that he giues it to whome
he pleafeth , and in diuers
manners .

Let her imploy as
much tyme to pleafe and
ferue God, as fhe hath done
to pleafe and ferue her huf-
band:

band: and by how much
the more she shall please
him, by so much more shall
she be happy.

Let her seeke to please
God with the beauty of her
soule, as she hath done before to please the world
with the beauty of her body: to wit, with her humility, chastity, wisedome,
loue &c.

In place of carnall &
worldly pleasures, let there
succeed spirituall, to wit,
prayer, reading, good
thoughtes, good workes,
frequeting the Sacraments,

Cc 2   hope

hope of eternall life, ciuation of the mind to God, & continual giuing of thanks to his diuin Maiesty. These and the like are the true delights and pleasurs of a true and vertuous Widdow.

Let her haue a speciall care, that the loue of riches, and Honours succeed not in place of the loue of her husband. For many haue there beene who haue vanquished and ouercome the lasciuious wantonnes of the flesh, and yet haue been themselues ouercome with couetousnes: and haue loued

ued

ued riches so much the more
disordinatly, by how much
they haue repressed the cō-
cupiscence, & desires of the
flesh.

Let her exercise her
selfe in all true vertue, as
well in her young age as in
her old; & as much as her
health and ablenesse of body will permit.

When she loues God
with her whole hart, all
kind of labour and toyle
seemes sweet and light.
And if it seeme pleasant vnto a hūter, to follow a wild
and sauage beast, with so

great

great labour, toyle, yea and danger of his life, to take him: what should it seeme vnto a soule inflamed with loue, to take paynes for the getting of God himselfe?

Let not a Widdow, though neuer so rich, noble, fayre, yea and though she haue neuer so fayre an issue of children, for this cause reioyce; but accompt her selfe as one desolate in this world; not relying vpon any other consolation, but wholy vpon God; esteeming her selfe but as a pilgrime vpon earth, banished

into

into this world from her
heauenly Countrey, & sub-
iect to many perils, and miseryes, a great way distant
from eternall happynes, &
most vncertaine euer to attaine therunto : And therfore let her lament with
King *Dauid*, & *S. Paul*, who
had the like thoughts and
cogitations.

If she do abound in ri-
ches, yet let her not set her
affection thereon . And a-
boue all things, let her con-
temne couetousnes and a-
uarice, the holy Scripture
saying : *There is nothing more*
C c 4 *perni-*

pernicious then couetousnes, nothing more wicked then the loue of money; since that for money the Couetous man will sel his own soule. And the Apostle sayth: *That couetousnes is the roote of all euil.* Our Sauiour also in the Ghospell telleth vs . *How hard a thing it is for those that be rich to enter into the kingdome of heauen: And that a Camell shall enter more easily through a needle, then a rich man into the Kingdom of heauen.* By riches are vnderstood all earthly things, and goods, disordinatly affected, or sought after .

When

When a widdow hath
done her deuotions, let her
neuer be idle; let her take in
her hand either wooll, or
flaxe, let her card, let her
ſpinne, let her wind the
yarn that others haue ſpon,
let her twiſt it, let her ſee
there be no fault in the
worke, and if there be any
let her mend it, & do what
is neceſſary . Being thus
continually occupyed, the
longeſt dayes will ſeem very ſhort & pleaſant : *For the
ſoule that is idle is full of bad de-
ſires*, as the holy Scripture
inſinuateth. And nothing
can

can be so pretious in the
sight of God, as to giue to
the poore the labour of her
owne handes.

Let a VViddow take
heed of adorning or atty-
ring her head with pearles,
Iewells, or pretious carca-
nets, nor vse frizeled hayre;
for these be the true signs of
hell-fire: but let her seeke
another sorte of pretious
stones, and weare them, to
wit, Humility, Feare of
God, and other vertues; to
the end, she may buy therwith that inestimable
pearle & margarite, Christ
Iesus

Iesus the spouse of the soule.

Finally let a Widdow vse discretion, maturity, & prudence in all her actions: let her consider who she is, & who he is to whome she hath consecrated her Widdowhood ; to the end she may obtaine his earthly benediction for her selfe, and her children in this world, & life eternall in the next.

CHAP. VII.

Divers memorable Examples of true VViddowhood.

VVE haue spoken already of the Famous

mous

mous and glorious Widdowes *Iudith* , and *Anne* the Prophetesse , before the cōming of Chriſt. Let vs now ſet downe ſome other examples . And firſt of all occurs that moſt noble and illuſtrious Roman Widdow *Paula,* of whom *S. Hierome* writeh , That ſo ſoone as her husband was dead , contemning the pompes & pleaſurs of the world, euen in the middeſt of ſo great wealth and aboundance of riches, choſe the ſtate of perpetuall Continency in widowhood .

Bleſilla

Blefilla likewife renowned for her beauty, wealth,
and honour, her husband
defceafing, & fhe being left
a young and noble Lady,
chofe the holy State of widowhood, by which fhe
became renowned to al po-
fterity.

Melania was no leffe
prayfe-worthy, who when
her husband being dead, &
not as yet buryed, fhe cau-
fed the bodyes of two of her
fonnes (of very great hope
and expectation, a little before alfo defceafed) to be
brought vnto her husbands

D d   body

body, where after extreme weeping, sighing, & drowninge of her selfe almost in teares, and euen loathing as it were marriage for the cares, troubles, & torments that it bringes, without any longer deliberation, consecrated her selfe vnto God, by vowing perpetuall Widdowhood.

Eufrasia likewise a Roman Lady is not inferiour to the aboue named, whose husband dying, she being in her young & flourishing age, fayre, noble, rich, contemned a second marriage, wher-

wheruto she was sollicited by the Emperour himselfe. And so dimissing her seruants and retinew, retyred her selfe into *Thebais*, where she liued most Saintly in perpetuall widdowhood.

The same did *Elizabeth* daughter to the King of *Hungary*, who being depriued of her Lord and Husband, presently contemned the pleasures of the Court, and vanityes of the world, giuing her selfe wholy to the seruice of poore, sicke, & needy people; not enduring that any man besides Iesus

D d 2   Christ,

Chrift , fhould be called her Spoufe, which fhe truly acknowledged in the poor.

The noble and moft worthy example of *Conftantia* daughter to *Cõftantine* the Great, Emperour , is admirable: who whileft her husband was yet liuing, deferued to receaue the crowne and merit of Continency. For that her Father the Emperour marrying her to *Halicarnus* Captaine of the Romen Army, fhe firft perfwaded him to be a Chriftian, afterward to giue ouer the warres, to lay afide his purple,

purple, and finally for the
loue of Ieſus Chriſt, to
vow perpetuall Chaſtity.

The ſame did *Chunegun-
dis* wife to *Henry* the Emperour, who perſwaded him
alſo to liue in perpetuall
Chaſtity, as ſhe had vowed
to do; whereby they both
became Saintes of Gods
Church, renowned to all
poſterity.

Neither muſt we paſſe
ouer in ſilence the moſt
worthy and noble example
of *Galla* daughter to *Simma-
chus* a Conſul of *Rome*, whoſe
husband deceaſing, and ſhe

D d 3   leit

lett a yong and beautifull widdow, was so assayled with infirmityes, that her body became ful of botches and soares. She consulted with her Doctours, who all agreed, that if she would be cured, she must marry againe. Whose counsell she so much disliked, that she sayd, She would rather endure the same all the dayes of her life, yea death it self, then marry againe: which purpose she truly observed most Saintly in holy Widdowhood to her dying-day.

An a

Ania also another Roman
Lady, and widdow of great
worth and nobility, yong,
& fayre, her husband being
dead, which he had enioy-
ed but a small while, was
earneſtly ſollicited by her
friends to a ſecond marriage, which ſhe vterly refuſed.
Being by them demaunded
the cauſe why, ſhe ſaid. If
(quoth ſhe) I ſhould marry
again, & find a good hubãd
like to my former, I ſhould
liue continually in feare to
looſe him by death : and
leaſt I ſhould chãce to light
vpon a bad husband, I will
Dd4   not

not aduenture vpon such
a disgrace. An act and purpose surely wise, and graue,
worthy to be considered
attentiuely by widdowes,
that desyre to liue out of
danger.

As nobly and prudently
did *Olimpia* of *Constantinople* ,
disciple of *S. Iohn Chrysostome*,
and the widdow of *Nebridi-*
us Prefect of the Army, a
man of most noble Re-
nowne, who hauing byn
married but twenty mo-
neths only, was exhorted
by *Theodosius* the Emperour
to marry againe , since she
was

was both yong, fayre, no-
ble, rich, learned, and held
of euer one for a virgin. She
made this Anſwere . If my
Lord the Emperour (quoth
ſhe) would haue me to marry againe , why did he ſo
ſoone depriue me of my
husband (for he was ſlayne
in the Emperours warres)
who was ſo agreable to my
nature , and myne to his ?
But becauſe his Highneſſe
knows me to be vnfit for a
marryed Eſtate, it ſeemes he
hath quickly deliuered me
from that ſeruitude : and
made me print in my hart
the

the delight of Continency
in widdowhood .

And let no man meruaile
that the continency of widdowhood is so much recō-
mended to Chriſtian wo-
men , ſeing that among the
Gentills , ſpeciaily the old
Romans, the ſame was ſo greatly honoured, that when a
widdow died, her head was
adorned with a Crowne of
Continency , and to caryed
in ſolemne triumph to her
graue .

The ſaid Romans did
also attribute another honour to the Continency of
wid-

Widdowhood, which was,
That on the wedding day,
there were no women suf-
fered to come neere, much
lesse to touch the Bride, but
only such as had beene the
wiues of one husband, to
wit, such as had beene but
once marryed; cōmanding
all that had beene twice
marryed (yea though they
were Widdowes) to keep a-
loofe of, as prophane, impure, and fortelling of an
euill fortune to the happynes of marriage.

They did moreouer ac-
compt it a signe of great in-
tempe-

temperance in any woman,
to marry more then once.
And for this cauſe one *Portia*
a Noble Lady being in cō-
pany of other Matrons and
Dames vpon a tyme; & vn-
derſtanding that one of thē
had beene twice marryed,
ſayd vnto her : *Madame*, *The
happy, and chaſt woman neuer
marryes but once* . A ſaying
worthy of a moſt prudent
and wiſe Lady. And con-
forme to this was that moſt
laudable fact of *Cornelia*,
daughter to *Africanus* & wife
to *Tyberius Gracchus* , who
when her huſband was deſ-
ceaſed

seased, refused a second Marriage with King *Ptolomey*, accompting it an act of too great Intemperance so to do.

And of no lesse praise & commendation was Continency in Widdow-hood, held amongst the ancient Iewes, in the old Testamēt wherof before we haue set downe the Examples of *Iudith* & *Anne* the Prophetesse, and so needlesse to be heere againe repeated.

The chast Continency also of that holy and vertuous Widdow of *Sarepta*, is

E e   not

not vnknowne, to whome *Meale* & *Oyle* neuer wanted during the tyme of that great famine, till by gods commandement it rayned againe vpon the dry and withered earth, wherbythe same became so moist and fertile, as it filled the Coun-treys round about with all aboundance.

CHAP.

CHAP. VIII.

*Of the works of Mercy, Deuotion,
Courage, and Constancy of
widdowes. And of the
Mantle, and the Ring.*

AMONGST many,
this is not the least,
nor last pious Consideration, that in all Countreyes
of Christendome, the noble workes and monuméts
of widdowes are yet extát.
Nor shall we need at this
tyme to trauaile out of our
owne Iland of *England*, to
view the same.

For it is well knowne,

that ther is scarle any Citty,
Towne, yea or Borrough
thoughout all England ,
without some monument
or other, of pious widdowes.

For how many goodly
Hospitalls , Almes-houses
Free-schooles , yea some
famous Churches also haue
you seene built , and endo-
wed with sufficient rents,
& reuenews by widdowes?
How many High-wayes ,
Bridges, Wels, Crosses, haue
byn made , and exected by
pious Widdowes , for the
increase of deuotion in the
people

people , and for the good of
their owne foules?

What Prayers , I pray
you, what Mortifications,
Téperance , Night-watch-
inges giuing of almes, haue the deuour Widdowes of
our Countrey in former tymes (and now a dayes very
many alfo, but yet not com-
parable to the former) exer-
cifed, for the loue of God ;
taking a true delight therin
in their moft Chaft Wid-
dow-hood, to ferue their
fpoufe Chrift Iefus, whome
they had chofen infteed of
their deceafed hufbands?

E e 3   How

How many of prime Nobility haue we had, in our Countrey, that haue contemned second marriages? And if we should recount all, we should perhaps surpasse the greatest part of Christendome basides, in that kind: some entring into Religion and becomming Nunnes, yea great Saints also; & others exercising workes of mercy at home among the poore, to the great comfort of the distressed.

And to begin with Queenes, how many I pray you

you, haue we had in our
little Iland, that after the
death of their Lords, haue
set aside all pompe and vanity of the world , vtterly
refusing a second marriage,
and haue either voluntari-
ly shut themselues vp in
Cloisters , there to spend
their dayes in prayer and
contemplation with God;
or els haue retyred to some
priuate place , continually
exercising themselues in deuotion and meditation of
heauenly thinges .

Before the Conquest our
Iland was more fertile in

this kind, as being neerer to
their primitiue feruour , &
that in few ages, thē it hath
byn euer ſince . For within
the compaſſe of 500. yeares,
there haue byn aboue thirty Queenes, that our Hiſto-
ries do make mention of, to
haue made themſelues cy-
ther Nuns in Monaſteries as
is aboue ſaid, or els haue li-
ned priuatly at home, con-
tinuinge in their Chaſte
widdowhood to their dy-
ing day .

Of the bloud Royall ,
and other Noble familyes ,
the number is far greater;
neyther

neyther will it be to our
purpoſe in this place to recount them all. Only this I
note, that the greateſt part
of the forſaid Queens (be-
ſides others of noble families) were many ages ago
accoūted Saints, & for ſuch
acknowledged throughout
Chriſtendome ; and many
Churches, Altars, and Mo-
numents of ſanctity erected
in their honour, and their
very Names famous to all
Poſterity. For to omit *S. He-*
len the Empreſſe, a Brittiſh
Widdow , and Mother to
Conſtantine the great the firſt
Chriſtian

Chriſtian Emperour, we
haue S. *Ermenild* & S. *Ermen-*
burge Queenes of *Mercia,* or
middle Engliſhmē; *S. Algiue*
mother, and *S. VVilfride* wife
to king *Edgar* the firſt Mo-
narch of England; *S. Edil-*
burge, & *S. Etbelwide* Queenes
of the *VVeſtſaxons; S. Eadgith,*
S. Ethelburge, S. Chineburge, S.
Ealſtede, S. Audry Queenes of
Northumberland; S. Oſith Queene of the *Eaſtſaxons; S. Sexburg*
Queen of *Kent; S. Hereſwide*
Q. of the *Eaſtangles; S. Aga-*
tha, widdow of Prince *Ed-*
ward ſurnamed the Outlaw;
S. Margaret Queene of *Scol-*
land

land , *Maude* the Empreſſe
&c.

All theſe, anũ very many
others, were moſt eniment
in piety & deuotion , both
in their widdowhood, and
continẽcy : yea ſome of thẽ
vowed chaſtity their Lords
and Husbands yet liuing,
as *S. Edilburge* Queen of the
VVeſtſaxons,&*S. Audry* Queen
of *Northunberland*; at whoſe
bodyes and reliques it hath
pleaſed God to ſhew won-
derous ſignes , and worke
many miracles to teſtify the
ſame; wherby they haue
byn euer ſince, and ſtill are
honoured

honoured for Saints thoroughout the world.

It was an ancient custome in our Iland (and the same continueth in some parts of *Germany* vntill this day) that in tyme of warre, plagues, famyne, or of any publicke necessity , there were in many Citties and Townes a certaine number of widdowes ordayned to watch & pray continually, night and day , in the Churches , by their turnes or courses , one or more togeather: because it was held, that their prayers were of more

more efficacy, and power
with Almighty God, to aſ-
ſwage his wrath, then the
prayers of other common
people, as perſons dedicated
wholy to his ſeruice, by the
obſeruation of Continency,
in their Chaſte, and Holy
widdowhood.

Neyther is the true Va-
lour and Conſtancy of de-
uout Widdowes, in our
Countrey, leſſe to be praiſed
and admired; ſince in that
kind alſo we haue gone beyond many other Nations,
eſpecialy in theſe later days,
when as their noble and
      F f   heroicall

heriocall Examples heerof
haue made them famous to
posterity; whether we respect their courage & con-
ftācy in suffering both losse
of goods & imprisonment
for their faith and religion,
as glorious Confessours; or
els the sheeding of their
bloud in testimony of the
same, as triūphant Martyrs.

For vpon some of these
widdowes hath God besto-
wed an inuincible coura-
ge and fortitude , ioyned
with an admirahle patiéce
in suffering for the Catholike Cause , not only im-
prisonment

prifonmēt of their bodyes,
but loſſe alſo of goodes and
fortunes, to their wholy
vndoing in their temporall
eſtates in this world, that
they might receaue a more
plentifull reward and me-
rit in the world to come.
And what Catholike in
England is there, that cannot witneſſe the ſame ſuf-
ficiently?

Vpon others, hath ſweet
Ieſus, of his infinite loue,
and ſuperabundant Cha-
rity beſtowed a more high
and ſupereminent gift, not
only in ſuffering, as is afor-

ſaid

said, losse of goods & liberty in this life; but also to scale the same with their dearest bloud, for his Names sake, Honour, Faith, and Religion . And this not vpon the meanest sort, but euen vpon some of the Bloud Royall of *England*; as is well knowne in the Lady *Margaret Plátagenet* widdow, countesse of *Salisbury*, and daughter to the Duke of *Clarēce*, in time of K. *Henry* the 8. & in the Soueraign Lady Q. *Mary* of *Scotland*, Widdow, and mother to our Soueraigne that now raigneth; vpon the

the deuout widdowes also
Ms. *Marg. Clitherow* at *Yorke*,
Ms. *Anne Lyne* at *London*, & o-
thers, in the late raigne of
Q. Elizabeth : All giuing
their liues for the constant
profession & defence of the
Catholike Faith, & therby
made worthy of a crown of
a Martyrdom, in their holy
widdowhood.

_____

Of the Mantle, & the Ring.

I T was also an ancient
custome in England,
(which I haue not read to
haue byn practised in other
Coūtreyes) for widdowes

Ff3   to

to weare a proper , and pe-
culiar vpper garmēt, called a
Mantle, by which they were
knowne, and diſtinguiſhed
from other people.

This *Mantle* was a lōg,
looſe Garment, which co-
uered them all ouer, & did
touch the ground, made of
blacke cloath ordinarily,
though others, who were
more noble, vſed them of
ſtuff, yet alwaysblack;ſigni-
fying therby that they wer
be accounted as dead to the
world, & to ſpēd the reſt of
their days in mourning for
their own ſins, & the ſinnes
of

of others, for whō of their
Charity they did pray.

It ſeemes that this cuſtome was in vſe in our Iland
long before the Conqueſt,
aboue 900. yeares ago. And
the firſt that I read of, to
haue brought in the ſame,
was S. *Theodore* Archb. of
Canterbury, ſent into Englād
by Pope *Vitalian*, about the
yeare 660. And a little after
him againe, by S. *Adelmus* Biſhop of *Sherborne* amōgſt the
VVeſtſaxons, who liued in the
yeare of Chriſt 709. of whō
it is recorded, that he gaue
hallowed *Mantles* to diuers,
F f 4   both

both Virgins & Widdowes
who had vowed Virgini-
ty & Continency: after the
taking wherof, it was not
lawfull for them to marry,
vnder payne of grieuous
sinne.

Afterwards, the same be-
came more frequent, & was
ordinarily vsed throughout
Englād, euen vntil this last
age of Schisme & Heresy in
the same. At the receiuing
wherof, were vsed diuers
pious and godly Cerimo-
nyes : to wit , that such
widdowes, as had for a certaine number of yeares, liued

ued in Contineney & widdowhood (after the death of their firſt husbãds only) & well proued themſelues therein , receaued from the Biſhop, a hallowed *Mantle*, kneeling before the high altar, in the Church, in tyme of ſolemne Maſſe ; as alſo a Ring of Gold , or Siluer, made plaine and round, like to a wedding-Ring, which was alſo hallowed . And this Mantle was put about their neckes , by the Biſhop himſelf, he pronouncing in the meane while, a ſhort prayer; as alſo the ring vpõ

the

their fourth finger, with a prayer likewise pronouced by the Bishop. After which, receauing the Bishops blessing, was songe *Te Deum laudamus*, in thanksgiuing; & the widdow thus adorned (with a veyle also ouer her head) was led home to her house by two graue matrōs, and afterward held and reputed for a sacred person, al the dayes of her life.

Nor after this, was it lawfull for her euer to marry, or to fall from this her pious purpose, without a most grieuous syn, & other Ecclesiasticall

Eccleasißticall punißhments ordayned for the same, hauing once receau'd that hallowed Robe, & Ring, as a pledge of her faith made to her Celeßiall spouse Chriß Iesus, by so publike and solemne a Cerimony of his Church

And we read, that about the tyme of K. Henry the firß, a widdow was seuerly punißhed by the Bißhop, for marrying, after she had receaued the Mätle & the Ring in the manner aboue sayd. Wherby it seemeth, that the cußtome was to make some

vow

vow of perpetuall Conti-
nency to the Bishop, at the
receauing therof ; and therby became subiect to Ec-
clesiastial power, & punish-
ment also, if she trangressed,
or sacrilegiously violated
the same.

FINIS.